Doing APOLOGETICS
with an African Mindset

Equipping Africans to defend the Christian Faith

EBENEZER AFOLABI

With the Word Independent Publisher

DOING APOLOGETICS WITH AN AFRICAN MINDSET
Copyright © 2019 by Ebenezer Afolabi
Requests for information should be addressed to:
With the Word Independent Publisher
210, Ebute Ojora Street, Ebute Road,
Ibafo Ogun State, Nigeria.
Email: ebenezerafolabi54@gmail.com,
Telephone: +2349050586045

This book is available at special quantity discounts for bulk purchase for sales promotions, premiums, fund-raising, and educational needs.

All rights reserved. No part of this book may be reproduced or transmitted in any form or by any means including, but not limited to, electronic or mechanical, photocopying, recording, or by any information storage and retrieval system without written permission from the author, except for the inclusion of brief quotations in review.

Unless otherwise attributed, scripture quotations are taken from the Holy Bible, New International Version. Copyright © 1973, 1978, 1984 by International Bible Society, used by permission of Zondervan Bible Publishers.

Published and printed in the United States of America by CreateSpace Independent Publishing Platform (an Amazon.com company), in association with:

With the Word Independent Publisher.

ISBN: 9781701078802

I LOVE AFRICA

Contents

Dedication..v

Acknowledgements..vi

Preface..viii

1. *Defending the Christian Faith in Africa*..........................13
2. *Understanding Apologetics and Polemics*......................24
3. *Biblical Basis for Defending the Christian Faith*.............92
4. *Brief History of Christian Apologetics*..........................102
5. *Purpose and Values of Christian Apologetics*...............109
6. *Branches of Christian Apologetics*...............................123
7. *Presuppositions of Christian Apologetics*....................127
8. *Current Challenges in African Christianity*..................135
9. *The Concept of God in ATR, Islam and Christianity*......142
10. *Who Do Men Say I Am?*..187
11. *Engaging the Intellectuals*..225
12. *The Jesus Africans Would Accept*...............................257
13. *My Recommendations*..267

BIBLIOGRAPHY..272

DEDICATION

Dedicated to my darling wife,
Pastor (Mrs.) Kikelomo Olawunmi Afolabi,
who has been my faithful partner in all things and heir
with me of the gracious gift of life.

And to our son, Inioluwa
growing so quickly
but still and forevermore
the delight of his daddy's heart.

Finally, to every lover of God in Africa.

ACKNOWLEDGMENTS

My special thanks goes to the Almighty God who is the source of my strength, joy and all that I have become today. To Him be all glory forever (Amen).

Special thanks to my wife, Kikelomo Olawunmi. She is incredible. She has always loved me unconditionally and has consistently supported me in all my endeavors.

My appreciation goes to my supervisor, Rev. Dr. Cletus C. Orgu—a worthy scholar and faithful teacher of God's word. He motivated me to get through with this work and provided indispensable insights and encouragement along the way.

Throughout this book I have used the study materials of Trinity Graduate School of Apologetics and Theology (A Calvin Research Group), and I have also quoted from the books of several authors. I am grateful to have had access to these materials.

I am also grateful to Professor Ebenezer O. Adeogun, my Apologetics lecturer at L.I.F.E Theological Seminary Ikorodu, for opening my eyes to the duty of defending the faith. The passion for this endeavor came into me when I came in contact with this course in the seminary, and the passion has not declined. Thank you Prof. Adeogun.

I also appreciate my loving and caring parents, Mr. and Mrs. Afolabi for their endless support and prayers for me. I pray that the Lord will tremendously bless them in return.

My sincere appreciation also goes to Reverend and Pastor (Mrs.) Olamakinde, for believing in me and giving me the platform to exercise the gifts of God in me. My appreciation also goes to friends and brethren who supported me financially for the publication of this book. Finally, to the members of Foursquare Gospel Church, Ebute Ojora, Ogun state, where I am privileged to pastor the people of God. Thank you for supporting me and believing in the call of God upon my life.

Preface

Christianity in Africa has recorded tremendous growth and transformation over the years. However, the proliferation of churches on the continent has brought both dignity and disrepute to the image of Christianity. Consequently, doctrinal disparities that exist among Christian denominations in Africa had given room to skeptics to question the integrity of the Christian faith, its doctrines, and ultimately the person of Jesus Christ. There seems to be an endless chain of *inconsistency* in what the churches in Africa profess.

Furthermore, there are three major religions in Africa, namely Christianity, Islam and African traditional religions (ATR). Although Africans do not have problem believing in the existence of God, but none of the three religions in Africa holds the same view about God, Jesus, salvation, life after death and the like. The point of disagreement between Christianity and the other dominant religions in Africa is always centered on God's relationship with Jesus (the claim that Jesus is the Son of God), the doctrine of

Trinity, and the divinity of Jesus. These are some of the reasons serious attention must be given to Christian apologetics in Africa, so that the uniqueness of Christianity amidst other religions in Africa can be established and doubters can be helped to overcome their doubts.

Without prejudice, African scholars will always be grateful to American and European Christians apologists, for their immense contributions to Christian apologetics and their efforts to save Christianity from all forms of doctrinal assaults and misrepresentations. Their publications, presentations, debates, etc. have greatly helped in putting things in proper perspective. However, it is regrettable to say that most of the publications from the American and European apologists were not written from the African perspective. Most writers of Christian apologetics do not write from the socio-cultural, socio-economic and socio-political realities of the Africans. This, *inter alia*, makes Christian apologetics as a Christian discipline to be unappealing to Africans.

Africa is the second-largest and second most populous continent on earth with an estimated population in 2016 of 1.2 billion people.[1] Unfortunately, the continent has been ravaged by abject poverty, social insecurity, terrorism, diseases, injustice, illiteracy, and other social vices. Therefore, the greatest need of Africans is *whatever* or *whosoever* could liberate them from the manacle of these monsters that have ravaged the continent for decades. For this reason, the need for Christian apologetics from the African perspective is very pertinent now.

The hopes of Africans are not dashed. Africans are very optimistic, but what should be the subject of our hopes and optimism is what Christianity preaches—Jesus, the hope of the world. However, the Jesus that Africans would accept and embrace is the Jesus who could identify with their experiences —the Jesus that will give peace and rest, the Jesus that will provide the basic things of life, the Jesus that will heal all diseases and give sound health, the Jesus that will defend the defenseless, and the Jesus that will protect and deliver from all spiritual and political oppressions.

---

[1] http://worldpopulationreview.com/continents/africa-population (accessed March 22, 2018)

More of *functional* and not ontological Christology is what Africans need and would appreciate for now. Therefore, the purpose of this book is: (1) to make solemn appeal to apologists to embark on the apologetics that will address the African experience, (2) (since Christian apologetics is not a popular Christian discipline in Africa yet,) to sensitize and convince scholars, seminary students, church leaders and Christian educators in Africa of the need to defend the Christian faith, through the presentation of the gospel in all its fullness and depth. According to F.F Bruce, "The presentation of the gospel in all its fullness and depth is the best defence against pseudo-Christianity...."[2]

There is need for contextual apologetics designed for Africans. As believers, the apostle Peter encourages us that we must always be prepared to give an answer to everyone who asks us to give the reason for the hope that we have (1 Peter 3: 15-16). This book is written to encourage African scholars, church leaders and

---

[2] F.F Bruce, *First-century Faith: Christian Witness In The New Testament* (Leicester: Inter-Varsity Press, 1977), 86-7

Christian workers to wake up to the task of defending the faith in the light of 1 Peter 3:15-16 and Jude 1-4.

Finally, I strongly believe that every apologetic endeavors must ultimately be *Christocentric,* Bible-based, Love-driven, and Purposeful. These four factors are what make apologetics a spiritual endeavor.

Ebenezer Afolabi

CHAPTER ONE

Defending the Christian Faith in Africa

Africans are inherently religious and they tend to see life not only from the physical, social and political perspectives, but also from a spiritual perspective. Unlike the modern-day Africans, the ancient African tribes do not separate culture from religion. They drew their moral values not only from their cultures, but also from their religions.

The modern-day Africans are slightly different in their thinking and worldviews from the ancient African tribes because of their exposures and education. However, there are several things which still connect the modern-day Africans to the ancient African tribes. One of such is the belief in the existence of the Supreme Being—the Creator of man and the universe. Africans also believe in the reality of the spirit world. Africans, whether modern or ancient, strongly believes in the reality of the spirit world. From the African perspective, the spirit world is populated with different spiritual beings. Before Christianity in Africa which redirected the focus of many Africans from worshiping idols to serving Jesus, each tribe or family in Africa have some deities or family gods they worship and pay obeisance to. They depended on these deities for protection, fertility, success and all kinds of fortunes.

Farmers would depend on some deities to cause rain to fall on their farms and give them bountiful harvests. Fishermen would have to make sacrifices to the river goddess so that they would not incur the wrath of the goddess and so that they can have great catch. They would attribute their successes to the benevolence of their gods and every misfortune is attributed to some evil spirits or it could be that the gods were not pleased with them.

Africans also believe that their deceased parents and other ancestors are alive in the other world. Those who hold this view still practice certain rituals to seek the favor of their deceased parents because they are believed to be alive in the other world. They believe the spirit of their ancestors or ancestresses will intercede for them, protect them, care for them, fight for them against every demonic assault and witchcraft oppression.

Africans also strongly believes in the existence and active operations of malevolent spirits, witchcraft spirits, ancestral spirits, territorial demons, spirit-husbands and spirit-wives, marine spirits and the like. Even professing Christians cannot pretend that these spirits no longer exist or they are no more in operation.

The only way non-Christian Africans defend themselves against these spiritual entities have been through uncompromising loyalty to their family deities and by fortifying themselves with amulets. On the other hand, in order to protect themselves from any form of spiritual attack against their health, their finances, businesses, and families at large, Christians would engage in intense warfare prayers, holding vigils every week to get spiritual strength from the Lord through prayers, going to prayer mountains to seek spiritual empowerment, and fasting for days and months as the case may be.

Apart from the above, the African continent have been ravaged with abject poverty, social tension, sicknesses and diseases, insurgences, abduction, injustice, corruption, insecurity, and illiteracy. Therefore, to defend the Christian faith in Africa, apologists must do so with consideration to the socio-cultural beliefs of the people and also understand their socio-political and economic challenges. This is the starting point to defending the faith in Africa.

The apologetic endeavor that will thrive in Africa must present the gospel and the Christ that can connect with the living experiences of Africans.

The Problems and Prospects of Defending the Christian Faith in Africa

The problem of defending the Christian faith in Africa can primarily be attributed to lack of understanding of the purpose and the operations of Christian apologetics. To buttress this, some think trying to defend the faith will amount to judging or condemning others. On the other hand, some also see Christian apologetics as an academic endeavor which is established to unduly scrutinize the spiritual import of Christianity. They argued that Christianity is strictly spiritual and no intellectual scrutiny must be allowed to challenge it. These are erroneous views.

Christian apologetics has no business condemning or judging others. Rather, its concern is to expose falsehood, refute errors, establish the truth, and to bring clarity to the gospel message. Put succinctly, Christian apologetics is first a spiritual discipline and not solely academic or intellectual display. It is spiritual because the Bible commands it and expects every practitioner to engage in it by first sanctifying Jesus as Lord in the heart. It is an intellectual discipline because it has to do with answering reasonable objections and this will require the use of reason.

Secondly, the problem with defending the Christian faith in Africa can also be traced to the misunderstanding of Christianity itself among professing Christians. This has led to the amalgamation of other religious practices and tenets with Christianity. Christianity is seen as a complementary religion by some professing Christians, hence, other practices that are totally foreign to the Christian faith was brought into it. For this reason, many Christians do not see the reason for defending the Christian faith, since it is a complement to other religions. Furthermore, another problem with defending the Christian faith in Africa is found among Christian leaders. Christian leaders, since they do not know too well, they cannot educate others to defend the faith.

The fear of being labeled a "critic" *inter alia* has also been discovered as one of the reasons why many Christians have been avoiding the task of defending the faith. The moment a particular idea becomes popular in the Church —whether it is erroneous or not —the church would embrace it and refuting it becomes a problem to many Christians in Africa, lest they are labeled "critics".

In addition to the above points, other problems facing Christian apologetics in Africa are the *indifference* of Christian leaders and lack of funds to push apologetic and polemic publications into the global market. Since the heretic teachings do not directly affect their congregations, and since the heretics are not propagating their heresies on their podiums, they feel less concerned. There is little or no support from Christian institutions and leadership for promoting the task of defending the faith.

Since there is still lack of understanding of what apologetics is and how it operates, little or no moral, financial and spiritual supports are given to it. Consequently, only few books have been published on the subject in Africa, and not too many media platforms have been deliberately created for the task.

However, with the introduction of apologetics as a course of study in Seminaries and theological institutions, there will also be a growing awareness for the need to defend the faith in Africa, and Christian apologetics shall be given a voice in Africa very soon.

The Practice of Defending the Faith in Africa

African scholarship is growing by the day, and scholars are making huge contributions to theological studies. Theological education in Africa is gathering momentum, but there is need to also create serious awareness for Christian apologetics too.

Many Church leaders are not really embracing apologetics because they are yet to understand its purpose. The common statement among church leaders in Africa regarding Christian apologetics has been, "let the weeds and the wheat grow together until the harvest" (Matt. 13:24-30).

Without undermining the diligent efforts of scholars in Africa, several moves have been made to curtail the erroneous teachings of some Christian leaders in Africa, through publications and theological conferences. Notable scholars like E.O Adeogun, Cletus C. Orgu, John S. Mbiti, N.S Nwigwe, S.O Abogunrin, Kwame Bediako, Abraham Akrong, Mercy Amba Oduyoye, Kofi Appiah-Kubi, Bénézet Bujo, Emilio J.M. de Carvalho, Jean-Marc Ela, Teresa Hinga, Kä Mana, R. Buana Kibougi, Laurenti Magesa,

S. Maimela, Ukachukwu Chris Manus, Takatso Mofokeng, J.N.K. Mugambi, Gwinyai Muzorewa, A.O. Nkwoka, Albert Nolan, Charles Nyamiti, Pashington Obeng, Efoé Julien Pénoukou, John Pobee, A.T Sanon, François Kabasélé, Harry Sawyerr, Cécé Kolié, Enyi Ben Udoh, P. N. Wachege, John M. Waliggo, Anne Nasimiyu-Wasike, Danny McCain, Douglas W. Waruta and host of others have labored and still laboring to bring clarity to the gospel message and to refute errors when necessarily.

Unfortunately, the publications of these scholars have only attracted few readerships. Apologetics has not been given a strong attention in Africa because of lack of understanding of the subject. The practice of apologetics as part of Christian discipline has been limited to theological environments and it only thrives among few scholars who knows and understands the need for it.

There is an urgent need for defending the Christian faith in Africa now because of the apparent amalgamation of contrasting doctrines that exists within the church in Africa. The Bible has become a secondary source of divine authority in some Christian circles and prophetic words from the lips of some self-acclaimed prophets are given preference over the Bible. There is also an overemphasis on *ecclesiastical paternalism* (pastors attempting to control the affairs of the flock and demanding respect and loyalty due to one's father from them at all cost) which needs to be curbed.

Also, there are over emphases on personal and extra-biblical revelations at the expense of biblical revelation. Furthermore, some church leaders deemphasized the sufficiency of Christ's death and resurrection by offering other alternatives to getting saved. All of these must be discouraged. To this effect, there is an urgent need to engage in Christian apologetics and polemics in order to deliver the gullible flocks of these heretic teachers from the snare of errors they have innocently walked into.

Apologetics is not optional for the Church. It is a *necessity* for every Christian to defend the Christian faith through every available means—the use of traditional media, social media, sound bible teachings, publications and establishment of sound theological institutions. It is not the exclusive responsibility of Christian scholars; every Christian leader and laities alike must be equipped for the task of defending the Christian faith.

CHAPTER TWO

Understanding Apologetics and Polemics

God out of His great love for humanity deliberately gave up His only begotten Son, only to be insulted, maligned, slighted, misunderstood, humiliated, and ultimately crucified like every other common and notorious criminal for the purpose of saving humanity. Likewise the Apostles; they were ostracized, hated, persecuted, and martyred for the course of the gospel and the Christian faith. With this understanding, the 21st century Christians must never allow scorners and ungodly men to bastardize, condemn, distort, criticize and freely attack the faith that was once delivered to the apostles and the fathers of Christian faith. It is high time for Christians in Africa to defend the faith by getting ready to always give answer to anyone who ask for the reasons for their hope.

However, defending the Christian faith must be with the motive of *establishing the truth* rather than wining arguments or making self-opinionated dogmatism to bully simpler minds. The Bible commands that defending the Christian faith should be done with meekness and fear—no matter how rude the attackers are.

Christian Apologetics and Polemics Explained

Matt Slick gave an amazing illustration of what apologetics is: Apologetics is like a field. In the center of the field is a garden. This garden has one door. Inside the garden is eternal life in the presence of God. Outside the field, however, are rocks, boulders, thorns, thistles, valleys, hills, and many false paths that lead nowhere. The apologist resides in the field and points people to the true path, so they can find the garden. The apologist seeks to remove the intellectual thorns and emotional rocks that prevent people from finding the true path to God. Also, there are many people who are walking false paths (cults, philosophies, etc.,) who will never reach that garden. The apologist gently guides the person, removes the obstacles, and points in the direction of the garden. When people arrive there, it is between them and God as to whether or not they enter.³

The term apologetics etymologically derives its meaning from the Classical Greek word *apologia*. In the Classical Greek legal system, two key technical terms were employed: the prosecution delivered the *Kategoria* (κατηγορια), and the defendant replied with an *apologia*. To deliver an *apologia* meant making a formal speech or giving an explanation to reply and rebut the charges, as in the case of Socrates' defense.⁴

Having explained the term apologetics from its etymological derivation, which signifies a defense or an explanation to reply and rebut charges, it is therefore very easy to define the term "Christian apologetics". Simply defined, Christian apologetics is the logical defense of the Christian faith. For example, the Apostle Peter wrote: "Always be prepared to make a defense (Greek, *apologia*) to anyone who calls you to account for the hope that is in you" (1 Peter 3:15 RSV).

---

[3] Matt Slick, *An Illustration of What Apologetics Really is.* http://carm.org/illustration-of-apologetics (accessed September 21, 2019).

[4] Ebenezer Adeogun, *Notes on Apologetics*, (LIFE Theological Seminary Ikorodu, M.Th. Programme, Ikorodu Lagos, February 2017), 11.

It is the conscious, deliberate defense and vindication of Christian theology as truth. It is not a kind of defense made on an empty ground but a deliberate, logical interaction with the critical criteria of truth in order to show that Christianity is real in its truth claims. Christian apologetics attempts to answer the question, "Is Christianity believable and rational?" It involves responding to false views by prevailing over them.[5]

Polemics explained

Just as the task of apologetics is to defend the Christian faith against attacks and criticisms, Polemics also carries the responsibility of defending the faith. However, both apologetics and polemics operate differently at some points, but there are several similarities between the two. Polemics, according to The New Schaff-Herzog Encyclopedia of Religious knowledge, "is a theological approach which is concerned with the history of controversies

---

[5] Afolabi, 33

maintained within or by the Christian Church, and with the conducting of such controversies in defense of doctrines held to be essential to Christian denominational tenets."[6]

The publication of Gay Christian Movement Watch has this to say about polemics:

> If the church does not engage in polemics to define the truth within its own ranks, then it will loss the current window of opportunity to bring the gospel to the lost. Failure to recover the authority of scripture will result in the culture's increased confusion, despair, and disintegration. Society will long for order more than truth and may turn to any source of authority to bring order. This situation could very well be setting the stage for the end-times Scenario taught in the Bible. This scenario will lead the world into a global government, economy, and religion.[7]

Obviously, the church is gradually drifting away from its fundamental teachings of faith and its core messages had been substituted for a somewhat "Social Gospel". Professing Christian leaders impose their own

---

[6] Ibid

[7] Ibid., 34

form of interpretations on the Bible and some wickedly relegate the doctrines of the Bible to a mere tale. Just for the sake of not appearing 'obsolete' or outdated, churches in Africa seems to be gravitating toward accepting the postmodern doctrine of inclusive faith—the doctrine which teaches that all religions are valid and that the exclusive claims of Jesus Christ as being the only way to God should be denounced.

There are lots of secular influences on the church today. Some Christian denominations in Africa have thrown the values of true Christianity overboard, retaining only the luggage acquired from the systems they have borrowed from the world. The most discouraging thing is the fact that those whose eyes have been opened to this apparent drift from the truth of the gospel proclaimed by the early apostles and church fathers have remained silent, indifferent, and apathetic about the situation.

No matter the case, the place of polemical defense should not be neglected or undermined because of the increasing secular influences upon the church and the prevailing quest for material acquisitions which had made many careless preachers and teachers of the gospel compromise their Christian faith.

Polemics provides the ground for the resistance of the heretic doctrines that had crept into Christianity in Africa. Its goal is to sanitize the church of every doctrinal impurity. Heresy should not be spared at all, but sentenced immediately to a perpetual silence and total elimination wherever it is discovered, because it moves faster than truth itself. Heresy is the opposite of orthodoxy. In other words, any opinion or doctrine that is anti-orthodox or that is contrary to the doctrines of the scripture is called "heresy". Engaging in polemics is therefore very important and must be given priority in the Church in other to limit the spread of false teachings in Africa.

1 Peter 3:15-16 and Jude 1-4: A Critical Explanation

The key texts we intend to explore as the bases for this discussion are 1 Peter 3:15-16 and Jude 1-4. These two Bible passages form the basis for both Christian apologetics and polemics. Therefore, understanding the above texts from the exegetical point of view will set this study in motion.

Text and Translation[8]

1 Peter 3:15-16 (*ΠΕΤΡΟΥ Α* 3:15-16)

15 κύριον δὲ τὸν Χριστὸν ἁγιάσατε ἐν ταῖς καρδίαις ὑμῶν, ἕτοιμοι ἀεὶ πρὸς ἀπολογίαν παντὶ τῷ αἰτοῦντι ὑμᾶς λόγον περὶ τῆς ἐν ὑμῖν ἐλπίδος, **16** ἀλλ ἀ μετὰ πραΰτητος καὶ φόβου, συνείδησιν ἔχοντες ἀγαθήν, ἵνα ἐν ᾧ καταλαλεῖσθε καταισχυνθῶσιν οἱ ἐπηρεάζοντες ὑμῶν τὴν ἀγαθὴν ἐν Χριστῷ ἀναστροφήν.

Selected English Version (NRSV)

[15] but in your hearts sanctify Christ as Lord. Always be ready to make your defense to anyone who demands from you an accounting for the hope that is in you; [16] yet do it with gentleness and reverence. Keep your conscience clear, so that, when you are maligned, those who abuse you for your good conduct in Christ may be put to shame.

---

[8] Michael W. Holmes, ed., *Greek New Testament: SBL Edition* (Atlanta: Society of Biblical Literatures, 2010), 462

Rationale for Choosing Text

One of the reasons this passage is important in this discussion is because this text forms the basis for which this book is written—the biblical foundation for Christian apologetics. In 1 Peter 3:15-16, Christians are not only enjoined to make a defense for their faith, they are also instructed on how to make such defense without compromising one's belief. The circumstances that surrounded the text also make it the relevant text for this subject.

While there are several scholarly discourses on how to go about defending the faith, this text gives a direct and simple method for doing such. However, the focus of exegesis here is to direct the minds of the 21st Century believers (clergies and laities alike) to the injunction to always be ready to make a defense for one's faith with gentleness and respect.

The Context

This letter claims to be written by "Peter, an apostle of Jesus Christ" (1:1), who also claimed he was "a witness of Christ's suffering (5:1). Although many modern scholars have disagreed with Peter's authorship of this letter and the place the author claimed he wrote the book if it were to be Apostle Peter, because the author claimed he wrote from Babylon. However, some scholars see Babylon in this context as a cryptic name for Rome.

The positive case for Peter's authorship, however, rests on these considerations: (1) the self-witness of the book is clear in claiming Peter as author. (2) The alternative of a pseudonymous letter by someone using Peter's name has serious credibility problems. (3) The church's early and strong reception of the letter as Peter's cannot be overlooked. (4) The letter reveals none of the tell-tale marks of a later writing in which the author ascribed his work to one of the apostles. (5) The letter makes good sense when taken at face value as by Peter; the content and tone are fully consistent with apostolic times.[9] In addition to the above, chapter 5:12 states that Peter wrote it "with the help of Silas. . .a faithful brother. . . ."

---

[9] Kenneth L. Barker and John R. Kohlenberger III. *Expositor's Bible Commentary* (Grand Rapids, Michigan: Zondervan, 1994), 1040

Scholars are also divided as to the actual dating of first Peter. Cheung states: "Commentaries offer arguments dating this letter to sometime between AD 60-68, and even 63-64."[10] Barker and Kohlenberger go for A.D. 62-64. They stated in their Commentary: "First Clement 5:4-7 names Peter and Paul as victims of persecution. The common understanding is that the passage refers to the persecution by Nero at Rome, which began after the disastrous fire in the city of Rome on July 19, A.D. 64".[11]

Some scholars find it impossible to reconcile the deadly persecution that followed with the admonition in 1 Peter 2:13-17 that believers are to submit under "every authority instituted among men" and to "honor the king." This is given as a strong reason for dating the letter to sometime before the great persecution under Nero, so that it must have been written before the great fire in AD 64.[12] However, Cheung maintains:

---

[10] Vincent Cheung, *Commentary on First Peter.* http://www.vincentcheung.com.pdf, (accessed June 26, 2017), 4

[11] Barker & Kohlenberger, *Expositor's Bible Commentary,* 1040

[12] Cheung, *Commentary on First Peter,* 4

But the argument is defective, so that even if the letter was written in or before AD 64, the above should not be considered a compelling reason to adopt the date. One of Peter's main points in the letter is that Christians should disprove the slanders against them by their good behaviour. And so the admonition to submit under the government is precisely what we should expect, as it is also consistent with what the New Testament teaches elsewhere (Romans 13:1-7). Except in cases where the Christian must choose between God or man, he is to be a law-abiding person of the land in which he resides.[13]

In 5:13 Peter indicates that he was "in Babylon" when he wrote 1 Peter. Among the interpretations that have been suggested are that he was writing from (1) Egyptian Babylon, which was a military post, (2) Mesopotamia Babylon, (3) Jerusalem and (4) Rome. Peter may well be using the name Babylon symbolically, as it seems to be used in the book of Revelation (see Rev 14:8; 17:9-10 and notes). Tradition connects him in the latter part of his life with Rome, and certain early writers held that 1 Peter was written

---

[13] Ibid

there. On the other hand, it is pointed out by some that (1) Babylon is known to have existed in the first century as a small town on the Euphrates; (2) there is no evidence that the term Babylon was used figuratively to refer to Rome until Revelation was written (c. A.D. 95); (3) the context of 5:13 does not appear to be figurative or cryptic.[14]

If, however, 'Babylon' is taken literally it may mean either Babylon on the Euphrates, or a place of the same name in Egypt, near Cairo. There are objections to both views. According to Josephus, the Jewish colony at Babylon had ceased to exist before A.D. 60. On the other hand, it is not likely that 'Babylon,' taken literally, would be used without qualification to denote any place other than the great city on the Euphrates. These difficulties confirm the view that we have here, as in Revelation, a mystical name for Rome.[15] Moreover, there is historical evidence that Peter was

---

[14] NIV Study Bible, *Introduction: 1 Peter* (Grand Rapids, Michigan: Zondervan, 2002), 1927

[15] James Hastings, ed., *The Speaker's Bible: I Peter, II Peter and Jude* (Great Britain: Speaker's Bible Office, 1924), 3

at Rome at the end of his life.[16] In AD 203, Tertullian wrote:

> Since, moreover, you are close upon Italy, you have Rome, from which there comes even into our own hands the very authority of apostles themselves. How happy is its church, on which apostles poured forth all their doctrine along with their blood! Where Peter endures a passion like his Lord's! Where Paul wins his crown in a death like John's![17]

Finally, Eusebius explicitly states that Peter wrote his first letter in Rome:

> The bishop of Hierapolis, named Papias [c. AD 60-130] . . . says that Peter mentions Mark in his first Epistle, and that he composed this in Rome itself, which they say that he himself indicates, referring to the city metaphorically as Babylon, in the words, 'the elect one in Babylon greets you, and Marcus my son'.[18]

The destination of the Epistle is clearly stated in the opening verse: 'exiles scattered throughout Pontus,

---

[16] Wayne Grudem, *Tyndale New Testament Commentary: 1 Peter* (Michigan: William B. Eerdmans Publishing company, 1989), 34

[17] Ibid

[18] Ibid., 35

Galatia, Cappadocia, Asia and Bithynia.' Hort suggested in 1898 that these names described a travel route to be followed by the bearer of the letter as he travelled through four Roman provinces south of the Black Sea, in what is today called Asia Minor, mostly in modern Turkey.[19] One may consider asking if the recipients of this letter were Jewish Christians or Gentile Christians. Grudem states: ". . .if all the churches in Asia Minor in AD 62-63 were reached by this letter and were the intended recipients of it, then the question of whether Peter is writing to Jewish Christians or Gentile Christians is already answered.[20] Since the letter was written over thirty years after Pentecost, and considering the exponential growth of the Church at the time, there could have been both Jews and Gentiles in the Churches Peter wrote to. Hence, the letter was addressed to both Jewish and Gentile Christians.

---

[19] Ibid., 37

[20] Ibid., 38

However, this letter was written in a time when persecution threatened. According to William Barclay:

> They are in the midst of various trials (1:6). They are likely to be falsely accused as evil-doer (3:16). A fiery ordeal is going to try them (4:12). When they suffer, they are to commit themselves to God (4:19). They may well have to suffer for righteousness' sake (3:14). They are sharing in the afflictions which the Christian brotherhood throughout the world is called upon to endure (5:9). At the back of this letter there are fiery trial, a campaign of slander and suffering for the sake of Christ.[21]

Peter clearly stated the purpose of his letter in the closing paragraph, "I have written to you briefly, encouraging you and testifying that this is the true grace of God. Stand fast in it" (5:12). His pastoral purpose was designed to sustain and encourage his Christian readers, whose "troubles are the ever-felt background of every paragraph.[22] Grudem adds:

> Since many of the exhortations in 1 Peter concern faith and obedience, it may be

---

[21] William Barclay, *The Daily Study Bible: The Letters of James and Peter* (Edinburgh: The Saint Andrew Press, 1979), 146

[22] D. Edmond Hiebert, *1 Peter* (USA: BMH Books, 1992), 28

suggested that the purpose of 1 Peter is to encourage the readers to grow in their trust in God and their obedience to him throughout their lives, but especially when they suffer. Peter accomplishes his purpose by pointing to what God has done for them in Christ, then applying that to the readers' lives.[23]

At the beginning of his valuable commentary on 1 Peter, Archbishop Robert Leighton writes:

> This excellent Epistle (full of evangelical doctrine and apostolic authority) is a brief, and yet very clear summary both of the consolations and instructions needful for the encouragement and direction of a Christian in his journey to Heaven, elevating his thoughts and desires to that happiness, and strengthening him against all opposition in the way, both that of corruption within, and temptations and afflictions from without. The heads of doctrine contained in it are many, but the main that are most insisted on, are these three, faith, obedience, and patience; to establish them in believing, to direct them in doing and to comfort them in suffering.[24]

---

[23] Grudem, *Tyndale New Testament Commentary: 1 Peter*, 39

[24] Ibid

Immediate Context (1 Peter 3:15-16)

Peter previously explained how a Christian can rejoice in his sufferings, having set forth his responsibilities and outlined specific conduct in times of suffering. He next emphasized the inner confidence a Christian can have when experiencing persecution for his or her faith, in order to equip his readers to overcome their sufferings effectively.[25]

In the thirteenth verse, Peter begins a new section dealing specifically with the problem of persecution by unbelievers. In the first sentence, the phrase "who is going to harm you if you are eager to do good" is a rhetorical question. It implies that harm is not the normal expectation, because those who do what is right should be rewarded and not punished for doing what is right. However, this is not always the case. Peter mentions the possibility of believers being persecuted for their faith. In other words, believers may suffer for righteousness' sake. Therefore, Peter's

---

[25] Thomas L. Constable. *Notes on 1 Peter*. https://www.ccbiblestudy.org (accessed August 21, 2017), 53

admonition here is centered on what should be the reactions of Christians when faced with persecution.

Verse-by-Verse Analysis

Verse 15: but in your hearts sanctify Christ as Lord. Always be ready to make your defense to anyone who demands from you an accounting for the hope that is in you;

Textual Notes

15. Κύριον δὲ τὸν Χριστὸν ἁγιάσατε ἐν ταῖς καρδίαις ὑμῶν, ἕτοιμοι ἀεὶ πρὸς ἀπολογίαν παντὶ τῷ αἰτοῦντι ὑμᾶς λόγον περὶ τῆς ἐν ὑμῖν ἐλπίδος,

In place of Χριστὸν the Textus Receptus substitutes θεὸν, with the later uncials (K L P) and most minuscule. The reading Χριστὸν, however, is strongly supported by early and diversified external evidence (P[72] אA B CΨ 33 614 1739 it[66] vg syr[p, b] cop[sa, bo] arm Clement), as well as by transcriptional probability, the more familiar expression (*κύριον τὸν θεὸν*) replacing the less usual expression (*κύριον τὸν Χριστὸν*). The omission of *τὸν Χριστὸν* in the patristic treatise *de Promissionibus* attributed to Quodvultdeus must be due to accidental oversight on the part of either translator or copyist.[26]

Exegesis

Peter, having admonished his readers not to fear, he gave them the antidote to fear: ". . . in your hearts sanctify Christ as Lord." Peter stressed the basic duty of making Christ supreme in the inner life (v.15a) and then set out supporting personal requirements for an effective testimony to the adversaries (vv.15b-16).[27] The Greek verb "ἁγιάσατε" which normally means to 'sanctify' or 'make holy' seems to have the sense, 'honor as holy, treat as holy or regard reverently'. It has a similar sense in Matthew 6:9, 'hallowed be your name' or better rendered as 'let Your Name be honored as holy.' As Clowney aptly remarks: "When the Lord sanctifies us, he makes us holy (1:2; 2:9); when we sanctify the Lord, we set him apart as the Holy one." The verb here does not mean "to purify, make holy," but "to treat as holy," "to set apart, enshrine as the

---

[26] Bruce M. Metzger, *A Textual Commentary on the Greek New Testament* (London: United Bible Societies, 1971), 691

[27] Hiebert, 225

object of supreme, absolute reverence, as free from all defilement and possessed of all excellence."[28] In other words, Peter admonishes his readers to put Christ above all other allegiances. In this passage, Peter once more ascribes to Christ the Old Testament name for the Lord. This is one of the important passages for Peter's Christology.

Peter goes on to encourage preparation for active witness which would win unbelievers to Christ. Peter envisages the need to respond to allegations of wrongdoing which Christians may face from their opponents, so he says: Always be prepared to make a defense to anyone who calls you to account for the hope that is in you. The word defense (*apologia*) almost always has a sense of 'reply to an accusation' (*cf.* Acts 22:1; 25:16; 1 Cor. 9:3; Phil. 1:7, 16).[29]

The Greek word *apologia* could mean to defend oneself, to speak on behalf of oneself or of others against accusations presumed to be false, to reason

---

[28] Ibid., 225-6

[29] Grudem, 153

with, to make a defense of one's opinions, positions or conduct, to give an explanation, to give answer to objections or to present proofs. The etymology of *apologia* (Greek: ἀπολογία) is derived from the root word *apologis* (ἀπολογὶς), "a speech in defense", and the corresponding verb form *"apologeisthai"* to speak in one's defense. The Greek philosophers Plato, Socrates, and Aristotle described *apologia* as an oratory to defend positions or actions particularly in the sense of a legal defense.[30]

Although some maintain that formal legal charges are in view here . . ., Kelly's point that 'always' and 'anyone' are extremely general . . . is well taken: whether to formal charges or informal accusations, Christians should be prepared to give an answer.[31]Ἀπολογία (followed by a dative, as in I Cor. ix. 3) means any kind of answer or self-justification, whether formal before a judge, or informal. Here παντὶ fixes the word to the latter sense. Λόγον αἰτεῖν' is a

---

[30]Anonymous, *Apologia*. https://en.m.wikipedia.org/wiki/Apologia (accessed August 11, 2017).

[31] Ibid

classical phrase. Every cultivated sensible man was expected by the Greeks to be prepared λόγον διδόναι τε καὶ δέξασθαι, to discuss questions of opinion or conduct intelligently and temperately, to give and receive a reason.[32]

Making a defense in this sense is applicable to every believer whose hope is in Christ. Opponents may request believers to give reasons about the hope in them, sincere inquirers may want to seek clarify and charge believers to justify the reason for their hope— the hope which makes them endure suffering and persecutions. Nevertheless, the object of believer's defense according to Peter is the "hope" that believers possess. Peter had earlier described what Christian hope is. Christian hope is real and objective.

According to Peter, it is a living hope, and this hope is founded upon the resurrection of Jesus Christ from the dead, and on the assurance that believers have an inheritance stored up in heaven for them—an inheritance that can never perish, spoil or fade (1:3-4).

---

[32] Charles A. Biggs, *A Critical and Exegetical Commentary on the Epistles of St. Peter and St. Jude* (New York: Charles Scribner's Sons, 1901), 158

The Greek word translated 'hope' in this passage is ἐλπις (*elpis*), from ἐλπω (*elpō*) which is a primary word meaning 'to anticipate usually with pleasure'. It could also mean expectation (abstract or concrete) or confidence. It occurs 54 times in the New Testament. Webster's 7th New Collegiate Dictionary defines hope as "desire accompanied by expectation of or belief in fulfillment."

Hope is often linked with faith in the New Testament because hope is the object of our faith. Hope is used in connection with eternal life (Titus 1:2; 3:7), salvation (Rom. 8:24-25; 1 Thessalonians 5:8), believers' calling (Eph. 1:18), resurrection from the dead (Acts 23:6), heaven (Col. 1:5), and also in connection with the gospel (Col. 1:23). Other words associated with hope are, faith and love (1 Corinthians 13:13), righteousness (Gal. 5:5), meekness (1 Pet. 3:15), joy and rejoicing (1 Thessalonians 2:19). 'Sorrow' is used in contrast to hope in 1 Thessalonians 4:13.

In his first epistle to Timothy, Paul states that the object of our hope is Jesus Christ (1 Tim. 1:1). However, "*elpis*" is also translated faith in Heb.10:23.

Some peculiar adjectives are used to describe the Christian hope in the New Testament. The Christian hope is:

a. Living (1 Pet. 1:3)

b. Good (2 Thessalonians 2:16)

c. Sure (Heb. 6:19)

d. Blessed (Titus 2:13)

e. Steadfast (2 Cor. 1:7)

f. Better (Heb. 7:19)

The possessors of this hope are:

i. Those who are in Christ (1 Thessalonians 4:13-14)

ii. Those who have been begotten (1 Pet. 1:3)

iii. Those who are justified by faith and by the blood of Jesus (Titus 3:7; Rom. 5:1; Gal. 3:24; Rom. 5:9).

In the final analysis, the duties of those who possess this hope are clearly stated in the Scriptures. Those who have this hope must rejoice in their hope (Rom. 12:12), purify themselves (1 John 3:3), wait (Gal. 5:5), be bold in speech (2 Cor. 3:12), remain steadfast (Rom. 5:3-5; Heb. 6:18-19), and must always be prepared to answer anyone regarding it (1 Pet. 3:15).

Non-Christians may be puzzled about this hope that they ask Christians to give account of this hope in them. It is therefore *imperative* for believers to always be ready and equipped to give answer (make a defense) for the hope in them. "Anyone" in this regard addresses every category of personalities. It could be skeptics or sincere inquirers. The type of questioning could be either official questioning by the governmental authorities as in the case of Paul before Festus and Agrippa (Acts 25:16; 26:2), or informal interrogation. Christians must be ready always to answer the questions regarding the hope they have in every circumstance.

Verse 16: yet do it with gentleness and reverence. Keep your conscience clear, so that, when you are maligned, those who abuse you for your good conduct in Christ may be put to shame.

Textual Notes

ἀλλ ἀ μετὰ πραΰτητος καὶ φόβου, συνείδησιν ἔχοντες ἀγαθήν, ἵνα ἐν ᾧ καταλαλεῖσθε καταισχυνθῶσιν οἱ ἐπηρεάζοντες ὑμῶν τὴν ἀγαθὴν ἐν Χριστῷ ἀναστροφήν.

Although the shorter reading καταλαλεῖσθε is supported chiefly by Egyptian (Alexandrian) witnesses, including p[72] B Ψ 614 cop[8a] Clement, it is to be preferred on transcriptional grounds, for recollection of the writer's earlier statement ἐν ᾧ καταλαλοῦσιν ὑμῶν ὡς κακοποιῶν (2.13) undoubtedly prompted copyists to modify the shorter reading by adding ὡς κακοποιῶν (syr[h with *] cop[bo?]) or by altering the person of the verb and adding ὑμῶν (vg arm (Speculum)) or ὑμῶν ὡς κακοποιῶν (ℵ A C K P 049 33.81 *Lect* it[65] syr[p, hmg]cop[bo?] eth *al*).[33]

Exegesis

Apparently, verse 16 is not meant to be isolated; it is the continuation of verse 15, stating how Christians should comport themselves when answering the questioners. However, there appears to be a slight problem with the verse division here. Textual variations exist among translations between the 15th and 15th verse. Some translations have ". . . But with gentleness and respect" as part of verse 15, while other

---

[33] Metzger, 691-2

translations have this at the beginning of verse 16. For instance, NIV, KJV and ASV have ". . . gentleness (meekness) and respect (fear or reverence) as part of verse 15 (although NIV and ASV has a conjunction and preposition 'but' or 'yet' and 'with' before 'gentleness' but only the preposition 'with' is found in the KJV, leaving the conjunction out), while NET and NRSV have this at the beginning of the 16th verse. A comparison between these two Greek texts reveals the variation.

Text from SBL Greek New Testament[34]

15. Κύριον δὲ τὸν Χριστὸν ἁγιάσατε ἐν ταῖς καρδίαις ὑμῶν, ἕτοιμοι ἀεὶ πρὸς ἀπολογίαν παντὶ τῷ αἰτοῦντι ὑμᾶς λόγον περὶ τῆς ἐν ὑμῖν ἐλπίδος, 16 ἀλλ ὰ μετὰ πραΰτητος καὶ φόβου, συνείδησιν ἔχοντεςἀγαθήν, ἵνα ἐν ᾧ καταλαλεῖσθε καταισχυνθῶσιν οἱ ἐπηρεάζοντες ὑμῶν τὴνἀγαθὴν ἐν Χριστῷ ἀναστροφήν.

---

[34] Holmes, Ibid

Text from the Byzantine Text form 2005 Edition[35]

15. Κύριον δὲ τὸν Χριστὸν ἁγιάσατε ἐν ταῖς καρδίαις ὑμῶν, ἕτοιμοι ἀεὶ πρὸς ἀπολογίαν παντὶ τῷ αἰτοῦντι ὑμᾶς λόγον περὶ τῆς ἐν ὑμῖν ἐλπίδος, ἀλλ ἀ μετὰ πραΰτητος καὶ φόβου, **16** συνείδησιν ἔχοντεςἀγαθὴν, ἵνα ἐν ᾧ καταλαλεῖσθε καταισχυνθῶσιν οἱ ἐπηρεάζοντες ὑμῶν τὴνἀγαθὴν ἐν Χριστῷ ἀναστροφήν

It is clear from the above texts that there are two slightly different readings between the 15th and 16th verse. The 15th verse of the SBL Greek Text does not have *ἀλλ ἀ μετὰ πραΰτητος καὶ φόβου,* but it is found in the 15th verse of the second Greek text. In other words, the 15th verse of SBL text has a shorter reading but a longer reading in the Byzantine text. The 16th verse of the SBL text begins with *ἀλλ ἀ μετὰ πραΰτητος καὶ φόβου,* but with *συνείδησιν ἔχοντες ἀγαθήν*in the Byzantine text.

However, this does not raise any serious theological problem. Since the original autograph does not have verse divisions, it is certain that the variations are

---

[35] Maurice A. Robinson and William G. Pierpont, *The New Testament in the Original Greek Byzantine Text form,* ed. 2005 (London: www.bibles.org.uk) accessed August 16, 2017

only found in the copies, and apparently two copies may not have the same reading of a passage. The textual variation does no harm to the content or the theology of the passage. What inspiration guarantees is the authenticity of the passage. Whether translators put ἀλλ ὰ μετὰ πραΰτητος καὶ φόβου, in verse 15 or 16, the author has made his point.

The apostle admonishes his readers to answer every questioner with 'gentleness' and respect or fear, as it is rendered in the KJV. Answers must be given with gentleness of attitude and behaviour, not being harsh with the questioners, but gently answering every objection—no matter how arrogant or insolent the inquirers are. Mentioned alongside gentleness is 'respect'. It is rendered 'fear' in the KJV, meaning 'reverential awe of God'. The 'fear' mentioned here is directed toward God while gentleness is directed toward man. Adam Clarke explains it thus:

> With meekness and fear. Several excellent MSS. add the word *alla*, but, here, and it improves the sense considerably: Be ready always to give an answer to every man that asketh you a reason of the hope that is in you, BUT with meekness and fear. Do not permit your readiness to answer,

> nor the confidence you have in the goodness of your cause, to lead you to answer pertly or superciliously to any person; defend the truth with all possible gentleness and fear, lest while you are doing it you should forget his presence whose cause you support, or say anything unbecoming the dignity and holiness of the religion which you have espoused, or inconsistent with that heavenly temper which the Spirit of your indwelling Lord must infallibly produce.³⁶

Cheung seems to have a contrary view of the words, "Gentleness" and "Respect" as used in this text. He maintains:

> The point that we need to make is that this context restricts the words, "But do this with gentleness and respect." The statement has been used to prescribe the proper attitudes, mannerisms, and even the vocabularies that Christians are to use when answering challenges from all kinds of unbelievers. Thus the verse has been reduced to something like, "Always be ready to do apologetics, but do it nicely." However, such an interpretation of the verse would condemn the prophets, the apostles, and even the Lord himself, as there are times

---

³⁶ Adam Clarke, *Commentary on the Bible: 1 Peter Chapter 3*. http://www.sacred-texts.com/bib/cmt/clarke/pe1003.htm (accessed September 16, 2017).

when they conducted themselves with anything other than "gentleness and respect" toward the unbelievers, at least as these words are now understood. Rather, they called the disobedient and unbelieving such things as whores, dogs, pigs, foxes, snakes, fools (or morons), hypocrites, wicked men, blind men, dead men, brutes, rubbish, dung, and so on. And do we need to repeat all the negative remarks that Peter himself has made about the unbelievers in this very letter that we are studying? On the other hand, the prophets and apostles usually answered *authority figures* with gentleness, doubtless "for the Lord's sake" (1 Peter 2:13) and acknowledging the fact that "there is no authority except that which God has established" (Romans 13:1). In one instance, Paul answered his interrogator with some of the harshest words possible, even with a curse, but he softened once he discovered that he was speaking to the high priest. . .Thus the strong tendency among apologists and interpreters to universalize 1 Peter 3:15 and condemn those who do not adhere to their standard of "gentleness and respect" is unbiblical (since it removes the words from their context, and distorts and misapplies them) and irreverent (for it indirectly criticizes the prophets, the apostles, and even the Lord). And I say that they use *their standard* of "gentleness and respect" because, whether in context or out of context, they do not use Scripture itself to define these words, but the non-Christian notion of

> social propriety. The result is that the unbelievers are controlling how Christians must deal with them. This in turn takes away the sting that is part and parcel of a biblical defense of the faith. It is not that we must be constantly harsh and insulting – that is not the point at all – but we must remain free to display the variety and intensity of expression as prescribed and exhibited by the relevant biblical commands and examples, and as necessitated by our encounters with different types of unbelievers. In any case, Christians should no longer allow teachers of apologetics to get away with the misuse of 1 Peter 3:15.[37]

Cheung's point does not in any way imply the harsh treatment of those making inquiries. Using his words, ". . . we must remain free to display the variety and intensity of expression as prescribed and exhibited by the relevant biblical commands and examples, and as necessitated by our encounters with different types of unbelievers."[38] Added to gentleness and respect is "clear conscience". The "clear conscience" relates to the liberty and boldness that come from living before God

---

[37] Cheung, 143-4

[38] Ibid

in purity (cf. Ac 24:16; 1Ti 1:19). So in the case in which non-Christians slander believers the statement of the truth may shame them into silence (cf. Lk 13:17).[39] Constable puts it this way: A "good conscience" is possible when we know our suffering has happened in spite of "good behavior," not because of bad behavior (cf. 2:19; 3:4, 6). A simple explanation of our good conduct may take the wind out of the sails of ("put to shame") our critics.[40]

Theology of the Text

The confessional theme of the pericope (1 Peter 3:13-17) from which the text of this discussion is taken bothers on Christian conduct under persecution. It highlights the blessing of suffering for righteousness and how Christians should respond in such condition, especially when asked to give account of one's hope. In other words, the passage teaches that faithful Christians need not fear those who are hostile toward them, but must be ready to make a defense for their

---

[39] Barker and Kohlenberger, *Expositor's Bible Commentary*, 1053

[40] Constable, *1 Peter*, 54

hope, knowing that God's blessings are on those who suffer for the sake of righteousness (vs.14). Therefore, the central proposition of the text is that Christian should expect hostility but react with meekness and respect.

Application

Just like the early Apostle, Christians must be willing and ready to defend the Christian faith. However, there is the tendency of being harsh and intolerable when faced hostility; Peter encourage believers to maintain the attitude of calmness, meekness, sobriety and respect when answering objections—no matter how rude the questioners are. It is also important to note that, since Christianity is not of any human origin, and the Christian faith is a matter of revelation, not human ideas, the apologist must know that no amount of logical presentations can lead any man to faith in God. No doubt, logic should not be dispelled; it should not be the hallmark of Christian apologetics.

Considering the Greek word employed for making the defense above (*apologia*) and its usage in other parts of the New Testament, the defense can be made in a formal or informal setting. The goal of Christian apologetics as a tool for the defense of the Christian faith is not to win an argument or impose Christianity on anyone; rather, it is to refute errors and establish the truth. It is also evangelistic in nature. Furthermore, all apologetic activity must ultimately be *Christocentric, Bible-based, Love-driven,* and *Purposeful.* These four factors are what make apologetics a spiritual endeavor. Therefore, defending the Christian faith is not an option for believers; it is a matter of necessity. The Church must be intentional about this task.

JUDE 1-4 (ΙΟΥΔΑ 1-4)

1 Ἰούδας Ἰησοῦ Χριστοῦ δοῦλος, ἀδελφὸς δὲ Ἰακώβου, τοῖς ἐν θεῷ πατρὶ ἠγαπημένοις καὶ Ἰησοῦ Χριστῷ τετηρημένοις κλητοῖς· 2 ἔλεος ὑμῖν καὶ εἰρήνη καὶ ἀγάπη πληθυνθείη. 3 Ἀγαπητοί, πᾶσαν σπουδὴν ποιούμενος γράφειν ὑμῖν περὶ τῆς κοινῆς ἡμῶν σωτηρίας ἀνάγκην

ἔσχον γράψαι ὑμῖν παρακαλῶν ἐπαγωνίζεσθαι τῇ ἅπαξ παραδοθείσῃ τοῖς ἁγίοις πίστει.4 παρεισέδυσαν γὰρ τινες ἄνθρωποι, οἱ πάλαι προγεγραμμένοι εἰς τοῦτο τὸ κρίμα, ἀσεβεῖς, τὴν τοῦ θεοῦ ἡμῶν χάριτα μετατιθέντες εἰς ἀσέλγειαν καὶ τὸν μόνον δεσπότην καὶ κύριον ἡμῶν Ἰησοῦν Χριστὸν ἀρνούμενοι.[41]

Selected English Version (NIV)
Jude, a servant of Jesus Christ and a brother of James, to those who have been called, who are loved by God the Father and kept by Jesus Christ: Mercy, peace and love be yours in abundance. Dear friends, although I was very easy to write to you about the salvation we share, I felt I had to write and urge you to contend for the faith that was once for all entrusted to the saints. For certain men whose condemnation was written about long ago have secretly slipped in among you. They are godless men, who change the grace of God into license for immorality and deny Jesus Christ our only Sovereign and Lord.

---

[41] Holmes, 479

Historical Background

In the Address the author styles himself "Jude, a slave of Jesus Christ, but brother of James." "Slave of Jesus Christ" meaning "faithful Christian," or laborer in the Lord's vineyard" . . . the second qualification marks him out as brother of that James who appears in Acts xv. xxi. as president of the Church at Jerusalem, who is called "the Lord's brother" by St. Paul, Gal. i. 19, and commonly regarded as the author of the Epistle of James.[42] Ordinarily a person in Jude's day would describe himself as someone's son rather than as someone's brother. The reason for the exception here may have been James's prominence in the Church at Jerusalem. Although neither Jude nor James describes himself as a brother of the Lord, others did not hesitate to speak of them in this way (see Mt 13:55; Jn 7:3-10; Ac 1:14; 1 Co 9:5; Gal 1:19). Apparently they themselves did not ask to be heard

---

[42] Biggs, Ibid., 317

because of the special privilege they had as members of the household of Joseph and Mary.[43]

Possible references to the letter of Jude or quotations from it are found at a very early date: e.g., in Clement of Rome (c. A.D. 96). Clement of Alexandria (115-215), Tertullian (150-222) and Origen (185-253) accepted it; it was included in the Muratorian Canon (c. 170) and was accepted by Athanasius (298-373) and by the Council of Carthage (397). Eusebius (265-340) listed the letter among the questioned books, though he recognized that many considered it as from Jude.[44]

According to Jerome and Didymus, some did not accept the letter as canonical because of the manner in which it uses noncanonical literature (vv. 9, 14).[45] Biggs insists: "Most of the commentators, whether they regard the Epistle as genuine or not, would accept

---

[43] NIV Study Bible, *Jude: Introduction* (Michigan: Zondervan, 2002), 1958

[44] Ibid

[45] Ibid

the forgoing explanation of the Address."[46] However, Jude seems so receive stronger attestation than 2 Peter.

The time of writing is very difficult to ascertain. Since Jude was a younger brother of Jesus, he may have lived into the second century. After the Jewish revolts against Rome in A.D. 66-70, Jude probably lived outside Jerusalem — and perhaps outside Palestine, if he was still alive. References in the text to the false teachers and the apostles (vv. 3-5, 17) suggest a condition in the church some years after the day of Pentecost. Similarities with Peter's writings have led some to date Jude about the time that Peter wrote. Obviously these are all very tentative guesses. Perhaps a date between A.D. 67 and 80 would be correct. At that time, Jude may have been living somewhere outside Palestine.[47]

Many scholars regard this epistle as an "epistolary sermon." Jude could have delivered what he said in

---

[46] Biggs, Ibid., 319

[47] Constable, *Notes of Jude* (Published by Sonic Light: https://www.soniclight.com, 2017), 5-6 Accessed August 21, 2017.

this epistle as a homily (sermon) if he had been in his readers' presence. Instead, he cast it in the form of a letter because he could not address them directly. Other New Testament epistles that are actually written homilies include James, Hebrews, and 1 John.[48]

The description of those to whom Jude addressed his letter is very general (see v. 1). It could apply to Jewish Christians, Gentile Christians, or both. Their location is not indicated. It should not be assumed that since 2Pe 2 and Jude 4-18 appear to describe the same situations, they were both written to the same people. The kind of heresy depicted in these two passages was widespread.[49]

The author clearly stated his motivation and purpose for writing this epistle. He initially desired to write to his recipients about the "their common salvation" (Jude 3), but the invasion of false teachings and teachers within the Church caused him to change

---

[48] Ibid

[49] NIV Study Bible, Ibid., 1958-9

his mind. He maintained that certain men whose condemnation was written about long ago have secretly slipped in among them. For this reason, Jude chose to address the issue of "the faith that was once and for all entrusted to the saints". Jude's goal, according to Bob Utley, "was orthodoxy, but he approached the subject through godly living (orthopraxy), not doctrine (very similar to James 2:14-22)".[50]

According to Utley, the author's purpose for writing the epistle of Jude is also to encourage believers to (1). Contend earnestly for the faith (Jude 1:3,20), (2) be prepared for mockers and false teachers (Jude 1:18-19), (3) build yourselves up on your host holy faith (Jude 1:20), (4) pray in the Holy Spirit (Jude 1:20), (5) keep yourselves in the love of God (Jude 1:21), (6) wait anxiously for the mercy of the Lord Jesus Christ to eternal life (Jude 1:21) (7), have mercy on those who

---

[50] Bob Utley, *Free Bible Commentary: Jesus' Half-Brothers speak: James and Jude*. www.freebiblecommentary.org (accessed August 23, 2017).

are doubting (Jude 1:22-23), (8) be assured of your salvation (Jude 1:24-25).[51]

Furthermore, Jude's purpose is to give a strong denunciation of the errorists. He evidently hopes that by his concise but vigorous exposure of them, the church will see the danger of their error and be alert to the coming judgment on it. Jude also wants to reassure the church that the coming of such scoffers was part of the content of apostolic prophecy. In last paragraphs, he calls the Christians to exercise their faith within the received common instruction.[52]

Verse-by-Verse Analysis (Jude 1-4)

Verse 1-2: Jude, a servant of Jesus Christ and a brother of James, to those who have been called, who are loved by God the Father and kept by Jesus Christ: Mercy, peace and love be yours in abundance.

---

[51] Ibid

[52] Barker and Kohlenberger, *Expositor's Bible Commentary*, 1119

Textual Notes

Instead of ἠγαπημένοις, which is decisively supported by P⁷² ℵ A B Ψ 81 1739 vg syr^(ph, h) cop^(sa, bo) arm eth Origen Lucifer *al*, the Textus Receptus, following K L P and most minuscule, reads ἡγιασμένοις. The latter reading, which is modeled upon 1 Cor. 1.2, was introduced by copyists in order to avoid the difficult and unusual combination ἐν θεῷ πατρὶ ἠγαπημένοις.⁵³

Exegesis

Jude gives two descriptions of himself: (1) a servant of Jesus, (2) a brother of James. It is certain that the first does not confer apostleship on him, but the expression of his humility and loyalty to the Master. The actual Greek word Jude used to describe himself as a servant is δοῦλος (*doulos*). Although δοῦλος is normally translated "servant," perhaps to avoid the generally offensive term 'slave', but the word does not bear the connotation of a free individual serving

---

⁵³ Metzger, 725

others. The most accurate translation for δοῦλος is "bondservant".

The apostle Paul used the same word for himself when writing to the Romans (1:1), Galatians 1:10, Titus 1:1, etc., to express his absolute allegiance to Jesus. Bondservant indicates one who sells himself into slavery to another. Exodus 21:1-6 gives a clearer picture of the word. It reads:

> These are the laws you are to set before them: "If you buy a Hebrew servant, he is to serve you for six years. But in the seventh years, he shall go free, without paying anything. If he comes alone, he is to go free alone; but if he has a wife when he comes, she is to go with him. If his master gives him a wife and she bears him sons or daughters, the woman and her children shall belong to her master, and only the man shall go free. But if the servant declares, 'I love my master and my wife and children and do not want to go free,' then his master must take him before the judges. He shall take him to the doorpost and pierce his ear with an awl. Then he will be his servant for life.[54]

---

[54] *The Holy Bible, New International Version: Exodus 21:1-6* (Grand Rapids, Michigan: Zondervan, 2000), 118

Like Paul, Jude is saying his ear has been pierced with an awl, signifying that he has committed his life to the service of the Master forever. A *doulos* is one who is a slave in the sense of becoming the property of an owner. As a bondservant, his pursuit is to see the will of his master fulfilled. He is totally sold out to the service of his master.

The life he lives is for his master; his dream is to please the Master. A bondservant completely surrenders his personal ambitions and rights to his master. This concept did not connote drudgery, but honor and privilege because it is by will and not coercion. Jude also describes himself as the brother of James. The James whom he referred to as his brother was also not an apostle. Jude did not specify which of the James he referred to here, but the general belief is that the James he referred to his the brother of the Lord. The reason he chose not to call himself the Lord's brother is not clear.

However, Clement of Alexandria in his commentary, which still exists in a Latin version, answered the question thus – "*Judas, qui catholicam scripsit epistolam, frater filiorum Joseph exstans ualde religious et cum scriret propinquitatem domini, non tamen dicit se ipsum fratrem eius esse, sed quid dixit? Judas seruus Jesu Christi, uppote domini, frater autem Jacobi."* . . . The sense is, "Jude, the slave, I dare not say the brother, of Jesus Christ, but certainly the brother of James."[55] After his personal identity, Jude focused his salutation on the recipients of his letter: "To those who have been called, who are loved by God the Father and kept by Jesus Christ."

This term is synonymous with "Christians" because they have been called out of darkness into God's marvelous light (1 Peter 2:9), and they are also "loved by God the Father" (1John 4:16). "Mercy, peace and love be yours in abundance" is typical of greetings in the ancient times, but Jude chose to use love instead of grace in his salutation.

Verses 3-4: Dear friends, although I was very easy to write to you about the salvation we share, I felt I had to write and urge you to contend for the faith that was

---

[55] Biggs, Ibid., 323

once for all entrusted to the saints. For certain men whose condemnation was written about long ago have secretly slipped in among you. They are godless men, who change the grace of God into license for immorality and deny Jesus Christ our only sovereign and Lord.

Textual Notes

As between ἡμῶν and ὑμῶν, the former is strongly supported by such excellent witnesses as p⁷² ℵ A B Ψ 81 614 1739 syr^{ph, h} cop^{sa} arm *al*, whereas the latter is read by only a few minuscule and by vg cop^{bo}Hilary Ephraem. The omission of the pronoun in K L P 049 *ByzLect* probably reflects a desire to give the idea a universal character.[56]

Exegesis

Jude tells his dear friends of the eagerness to write on the subject of salvation and his reason for changing his mind. His initial plan was to write a letter which bothers on the doctrine of salvation. "The salvation we

---

[56] Ibid

share" or as rendered in the KJV, "our common salvation" speaks of that which all Christians now participate in. This is either referring to salvation in its present sense or in its future sense. Both are applicable here. However, whether Jude was actively engaged in writing or he was still thinking about it is not clear here. The manner at which Jude expressed his intention in verse 3 shows a sense of urgency and compulsion. C.G Brewer asserts:

> Jude intimated that he was writing under compulsion. He had been giving all diligence to this matter. This indicates that he was reluctant to write and that he had been considering it thoughtfully and prayerfully, but he felt *constrained* to write this Epistle. The fact that he made the Epistle very short shows that he was not afflicted with the *mania scribendi*. He wrote only what was necessary but he covered a wide field in these short verses. He had something to say and felt impelled by the importance of his message and by the exigency of the moment to say it.[57]

---

[57] C. G Brewer, *Contending for the Faith* (Tennessee: Gospel Advocate Company, 1941), 16

By saying "I felt I had to write," Jude explains that a compelling obligation to the people of God prompted him to change his focus for their spiritual good. His letter is now intended to exhort the readers to struggle for "the faith that was once for all entrusted to the saints."[58] Jude urged the recipients of his letter to contend for the faith that was once for all entrusted to the saints. The verb ἐπαγωνίζομαι (earnestly contend for) is an intensive form of *αγωνίζομαι,* and it expresses the notion of struggling, fighting, or contending for something, but this notion seems to have been heightened here. The verb used here suggests a continuous struggling or contending for the faith.

To 'contend earnestly for' (*epagonizesthai*) is an expressive compound infinitive which appears only here in the New Testament. The simple form of the verb (*agonizomai*), which appears as 'agonize' in its English form, was commonly used in connection with the Greek stadium to denote a strenuous struggle to

---

[58] Barker and Kohlenberger, *Expositor's Bible Commentary,* 1120

overcome an opponent, as in a wrestling match. It was also used more generally of any conflict, contest, debate, or lawsuit. Involved is the thought of the expenditure of all one's energy in order to prevail.[59]

The term "faith" has variety of meanings in the New Testament. Many Christian writers and theologians have tried to differentiate the various meanings of faith used in the New Testament, but in all cases, the context in which the word is used strongly determines its meaning. In this particular context, faith refers to the doctrinal content of Christianity which has been embraced by believers. It is not referring to the act of believing as some writers and preachers would make many believe. To this faith (the doctrinal content of Christianity), Jude urges believers to contend for. Biggs describes this faith: ". . . a body of doctrine, dogmatic and practical, which is given to them by authority, is fixed and unalterable, and well known to all Christians."[60]

---

[59] Constable, *Jude*, 8

[60] Biggs, Ibid., 325

Jude stresses that this faith has been entrusted "once for all" to the "saints." The saints here refer to those set apart by God for Himself — the Church, but more specifically the Apostles. Biggs raises a concern about Jude's language about the Faith. According to Biggs, "Jude's language about the Faith is highly dogmatic, highly orthodox, and highly zealous. His tone is that of a bishop of the fourth century. The character may be differently estimated, but its appearance at this early date, before Montanism and before Gnosticism is of great historical significance. Men who used such phrases believed passionately in a Creed." However, the faith to which Jude urged his recipients to contend for is fundamental, and its foundational truths are not negotiable, because it was delivered to the saints once for all.

In the fourth verse, Jude explains his motivation for writing this letter. It reads: "For certain men whose condemnation was written about long ago have secretly slipped in among you. They are godless men, who change the grace of God into license for immorality and deny Jesus Christ our only sovereign and Lord." According to Jude, these ungodly men have secretly slipped in among the believers. The Greek word used to describe the manner at which they came into the church is *pareisduō*, meaning "to enter secretly," "to slip in stealthily." They must have disguised themselves in order to gain access into the church without disclosing their true characters. Jude asserts that the condemnation of these men "was written about long ago." This phrase could refer to God's writing down from eternity the destiny (i.e., reprobation) of the wicked, but more likely it refers to previously written predictions about the doom of the apostates.[61]

After stating the destiny of these men, Jude describes them as "ungodly" or impious" . . . a term often used of notorious sinners. This general word is made more specific by the two charges that follow. (1) They "change the grace of our God into a license for immorality." Evidently their understanding of grace and perhaps of the forgiveness of sin led them to feel

---

[61] Barker and Kohlenberger, *Expositor's Bible Commentary*, 1120

free to indulge in all forms of sexual depravity. (2) They "deny Jesus Christ our only Sovereign and Lord" (2Pe 2:1).[62] Exactly how they denied Jesus Christ, Jude did not say.

Certainly they denied him by immoral living that ran counter to his commands. Perhaps they also denied him in teaching a Christology that denied either his full humanity or his full deity. However, the word translated "Sovereign" is commonly used of the Father (Lk. 2:29; Ac 4:24), and the word "only" makes it difficult to apply this word to Jesus. Thus this phrase can also be translated, "the only Sovereign [the Father] and our Lord Jesus Christ. If this is adopted, then the error of the godless men was moral rather than theological (cf. Tit 1:16).[63] Brewer gives a further explanation for the characters and teachings of these false teachers:

> They turned the grace of "God into lasciviousness." This means that they claimed license to indulge the flesh. Peter speaks of

---

[62] Ibid., 1120-1

[63] Ibid

these same false teachers, declaring that they led Christians astray by promising them liberty. (2 Pet. 2: 19.) They based this license on the grace of God. This means that they claimed since we had been freed from law and are now under grace (Rom. 6: 14) we are free to commit the sins that were prohibited by the law. There was a class of men in the early church who made this argument. These men are refuted by Peter and Paul as well as by Jude. In history these men were called Antinomians. This means "against law." But it is not probable that the teachers to whom Jude refers were of this class. Jude's false teachers denied the Lord Jesus, and therefore they did not claim that his grace had made us free. These men evidently emphasized the fact that God is *love,* and therefore he would not punish men for sin. They claimed that he is too good to inflict punishment upon his children, and thus they based their claim of exemption from punishment upon God's grace and goodness. Lasciviousness means lust or lewdness. These false teachers, therefore, were corrupt men and spread immorality among those who came under their influence.[64]

From Jude's description of these men, it is clear that they have been part of the church liturgy, and must have been teaching in the church. Jude's

---

[64] Brewer, Ibid., 22

description of the activities of these false teachers reveals a willful denial and perversion of the truth. These men were apostates. They became apostates because they willfully turned away from the truth. Apostasy is the obvious rejection of the truth.

The Bible uses many verbs to express the idea of apostasy. Among them, "turn away" (Matt. 24:10), "go out" (1 John 2:19), "forsake" (Deut. 31:16), and "rebel" (Eze. 2:3). The Hebrew term closest to our term "apostasy" is *meshûbah*. It is based on the verb *shûb*, which means "to turn." This verb is used, on one hand, to express the idea of repentance as a "turning" or "returning" to the Lord.

On the other hand a person who "turns away" from the Lord commits *meshûbah*, apostasy. Apostasy could be the result of accepting the spurious beliefs of false teachers (1 Tim. 4:1) or going back to the corrupting lifestyle of the world (2 Peter 2:20-22). It could also be the result of persecution (Matt. 24:9, 10), an unbelieving heart (Heb. 3:12), superficial commitment to Christ (1 John 2:19), and not paying attention to

God's Word (Heb. 2:1).[65]These false teachers perverted the truth of the Christian faith and taught others to do the same. They were antinomians, who used the grace of God as license for their immoral acts. Jude therefore urged believers to *contend for the faith* that was once for all delivered to the saints, lest these false teachers they succeed in leading the elect away from the truth.

Theology of the Text

With the sense of urgency and responsibility, Jude wrote to encourage believers to contend for the faith, because of the presence of false teachers in the church. His concern was to ensure that the truth of the Christian faith is not perverted by the false teachers. To achieve this goal, Jude vigorously exposed the false teachers, stating clearer who they are and what they do. Furthermore, Jude maintains that the doctrinal content of the Christian faith gives no room for any replacement or embellishment. The faith that was once for all delivered to the saints is a "fixed" core of truth, and no room must be created for the mixture of

---

[65]Ángel Manuel Rodríguez, *What is Apostasy?* (Biblical Research Institute General Conference of Seventh-day Adventists), 1

error with the truth. Jude also reminds his readers of the impending judgment of God on anyone who perverts the truth. Finally, Jude stands against any attempt to compromise God's once-and-for-all disclosure of Jesus.

Application

Just like Jude, believers and all Christian leaders should express their allegiances to the truth by exposing falsehood and speaking vehemently against any perversion of the Christian faith. This faith that was once for all delivered to the saints was passed down from one generation to the other because some men contended for the faith.

It is unfortunate that most Christian leaders of my time have lost the courage to defend the faith. Some are indifferent and apathetic about the task and consequently, false teachers are subtly making their ways into the fold. The 21st century believers and Church leaders seem to have given these erroneous teachers access into the Church and they offer them stages to pour forth their erroneous teachings. Silence is sometimes taken for consent; therefore, the silence of Church leaders in Africa has further promoted the enterprise of these false teachers. In the sentiment of Benjamin Franklin, who believed, "As we must account for every idle word, so we must for every idle silence." Ray Stedman stated:

> Now some think that contending for the faith means to roll the Bible up into a bludgeon with which to beat people over the head. Such people feel that they need to be very contentious in contending for the faith. But this is not what Jude has in mind at all. He is simply talking about the need for proclaiming the truth. As Charles Spurgeon used to put it: "The truth is like a lion. Whoever heard of defending a lion? Just turn it loose and it will defend itself." This is the way the word of God is. If we begin to proclaim it, it will defend itself.[66]

John Piper also added his thought:
> At least two things are evident here. One is that contending sometimes involves an intellectual effort to change the way a person thinks: "Convince some who doubt." The other is that contending sometimes involves moral reclamation: go after them into the mess where

---

[66]Ray Stedman, *Contending for the Faith*. http://www.sermoncentral.com (accessed August 31, 2017)

there perverse ideas have taken them, and snatch them back to safety even while you hate what they are doing.[67]

The Implications of 1 Peter 3:15-16 and Jude 1-4 for Christianity in Africa

By implication, I mean the 'effect' or 'consequence' of 1 Peter 3:15-16 and Jude 1-4 for Christianity in Africa. Without prejudice, religious syncretism has become the major part of Christianity in Africa. Consequently, many Christians and non-Christians are no longer sure of what they should believe or should not believe about the Bible and the Christian faith. Extra-biblical revelations are becoming rampant and receiving more recognition by the day. The Bible is almost becoming the secondary source of authority in the church and many other *pseudo-Christian* practices are also getting popular. A particular observer made this remark about African Christianity: "African Christianity is wide in its scope but it is one inch deep." This is true to some extent. Therefore, Church leaders in Africa needs to vehemently re-echo and put

---

[67] John Piper, *Contending for the Faith*, Ibid

into practice, the words of Apostle Peter and Jude both on the pulpit and in all available media platforms.

The implications of taking 1 Peter 3:15-16 and Jude 1-4 seriously in Africa is that, it will minimize the apparent manipulations of Christian doctrines present in the church of Africa and help to expose the heretics in the church and also deliver the laities from religious deceptions.

Furthermore, if every Christian leader, pastors, Sunday school teachers, seminarians, and other ministers would take to the words of the apostle Peter and Jude, it will put a check on those promulgating falsehood and minimize their activities also.

Some of the ministers who promulgate these falsehoods do so out of ignorance and wrong biblical interpretations. They do so because they lack theological training. No matter the circumstance, their activities should also be checked and they should be cautioned with respect and gentleness. However, there are many other promulgators of falsehood in the church who do so willfully, out of disloyalty to the scriptures, and for selfish reasons. 1 Peters 3:15-16 and Jude 1-4 instructs African scholars and church leaders to actively and proactively stand against such manipulation of the truth.

Nevertheless, the instructions in 1 Peter 3:15-16 and Jude 1-4 does not imply defending the faith against attacks outside the church (apologetics) only, but also the defense of the Christian faith against those who distorts the truth of the Christian faith from within the church (polemics). Africa needs the emergence of both apologists to deal with the attacks coming from outside the church and also polemicists who are equipped to deal with the spread of heretical teachings within the church. Guinness maintains:

> If the church does not engage in polemics to define the truth within its own ranks, then it will loss the current window of opportunity to bring the gospel to the lost. Failure to recover the authority of scripture will result in the culture's increased confusion, despair, and disintegration. Society will long for order more than truth and may turn to any source of authority to bring order. This situation could very well be setting the stage for the end-times scenario taught in the Bible. This scenario will

lead the world into a global government, economy, and religion.[68]

Defending the Christian faith is best done within the context of Christian apologetics. This is so because Christian apologetics is an interdisciplinary subject dealing with various opposing views against the Christian faith. Christian apologetics could interact with philosophy, history, ethics, history, theology, science and archeology.

Sceptics and secular scholars demand that Christians should provide verifiable proofs for their claims, and unbelievers have made several attempts to also engage believers in some difficult discussions which often leave them in the state of confusion, depression, doubt and feelings of incompetence. They (unbelievers) place more emphasis on Bible difficulties and they take advantage of some Christians' inabilities to intelligently defend the Christian faith and provide adequate answers to the questions they throw at them.

---

[68] Guinness, Ibid

Consequently, this leaves some Christians with a split mentality because they are unable to defend their faith. Therefore, studying apologetics or having a little background in apologetics will help a Christian who finds himself in a split mentality to solidify his faith and help others who already doubt their faith to overcome their doubts.

Christian leaders must wake up to the task of defending the Christian faith and using the very word of Jude, they should "earnestly contend for the faith" with all passion, by first showing their allegiances to the truth and their commitments to the Christian faith. They should acquire different methods and technics for doing so, without compromising the truth themselves. Therefore, it is imperative for them to first of all *know what they believe* and *who they believe.* The use of literature, mass and social media, deliberate teachings on the doctrines of the Bible and other means of communication will be appropriate for the task.

Having acquired the skills for defending the faith, Church leaders *must* educate their congregations, from childhood to adulthood, on how to detect errors for themselves, by teaching them the sound doctrine of the Bible and also teaching them to know *what they believe, what to believe* and *who they believe.* This will in the long run help believers to contend for the faith and remain steadfast in the faith.

Finally, taking to Peter's and Jude's advice to defend and earnestly contend for the faith will help to preserve and transmit the tradition of truth in Africa, so that the errors of this generation are not passed down to the coming generations.

Reasons to Engage in Christian Apologetics

Having examined the two pivotal texts for this study (1 Peter 3:15-16 and Jude 1-4), we have the following reasons to engage in Christian apologetics:

1. The Bible command it (1 Peter 3:15, 16).

2. Engaging in apologetics helps in the removal of intellectual and emotional barriers to receiving the Christian faith.

3. It helps to provide answers to questions asked by sincere inquirers.

4. It strengthens our faith and equips us for future attacks against the Christian faith.

5. The Apostles and the early church fathers also engaged in apologetics. They therefore become our examples.

6. Apologetics helps to correct those who are erring from the Biblical truth.

7. Apologetics provide appropriate information to clarify the authenticity of the Christian faith.

The Attitude of Christian Apologist

The exegesis of 1 Peter 3:15-16 and Jude 1-4 provides a template for the attitudes Christian apologists must put up in when defending the faith:

1. Respect
2. Decency
3. Gentleness
4. Meekness
5. Conviction
6. Courage
7. Diligence
8. Cheerfulness

9. Sincerity

10. Firmness

11. Moral uprightness

12. Openness of mind

12. Dependence on the Holy Spirit

Read the following Bible texts for further learning: 2 Tim. 2:24; Philippians 1:27; Acts 24:18; 24:10.

The Motivations of a Christian Apologist

1. Concern for the truth. The primary motivation of a Christian apologist is to see that the truth of the Christian faith prevails over falsehood.

2. Commitment to the truth. In addition to his concern for the truth, the apologist must also be committed to the truth of the Christian faith, by seeking to preserve and transmit the tradition of truth to other believers.

3. Communication of the truth. A Christian apologist must be conscientious in the delivery of his duty as an apologist, his claims must be consistent with the overall truth of the Christian faith, and he must present his case comprehensively and courageously. The motivation of a Christian apologist is to communicate the truth without compromise to sincere inquirers who would also communicate the same to others.

CHAPTER THREE

Biblical Basis for Defending the Christian Faith

It has already been established that Christian Apologetics is that branch of Christian studies that deals with the defense of the Christian faith. This is fully a biblical activity and not just a mere human idea. As the scripture commands: "Always be prepared to make a defense to anyone who calls you to account for the hope that is in you" (I Pet. 3:15 RSV). This implies that defending the Christian faith is one of the spiritual duties of believers in Christ. However, Apologetic activities in the scriptures in not only limited to the New Testament believers but it has also been demonstrated in the Old Testament.

Apologetics in the Old Testament

Several heroes in the Old Testament were confronted with the situations which demanded the proof of their faith and their assurance in the Almighty God. Necessity was placed on them to defend the truthfulness, reliability and the mightiness of their God. They were brought face to face with situations which demanded that they should defend what they believed. Doubters and scoffers sometimes challenged them and made mockery of their faith. To this effect, apologetic activities were demonstrated at various places in the Old Testament and this gives us a comfortable ground in the Old Testament.

In the Pentateuch (Genesis to Deuteronomy)

In the Pentateuch, when God commanded Moses to go to Pharaoh, He gave two signs to Moses so that he could establish that it was God who sent Him. The fact that God provided demonstration when Pharaoh asked for it cannot be denied. Through the hand of Moses God provided several proofs of His awesomeness and His ability to deliver His people from their enemies and bring them to the land He promised them.

In the Prophets

Another great example of apologetics in the Old Testament can be seen in the encounter of Elijah with the prophets of Baal. There was the need for Prophet Elijah to proof and defend the supremacy of the God of Israel over every other pagan gods (I kings 18:16-39). Apart from Elijah the prophet, many other Old Testament prophets stood to defend the integrity and the justice of the God of Israel.

In the Poetic Books (Job to Songs of Solomon)

In the face of opposition from his friends and family, Job attempted to vindicate the reason for his loyalty and confidence in the Lord. He makes it clear that the God he serves is not like the pagan gods around them. He maintains that his God is faithful and He will never fail those who trust in Him. Psalms 14, 19 and 24 are also apologetic in character. The actual number of apologetic passages and incidents in the Old Testament is too numerous to be listed here. For instance, Psalms 19 and 24 attests to the fact that God created the universe.

It is no doubt that Apologetics is implicit throughout the Old Testament. O.S Guinness traced its roots back to the fall itself and show how the Old Testament is an object lesson in using different methods of communication appropriate for the listeners.

Guinness gives some conclusions from the Old Testament evidences:

1. The greater the resistance and hostility, the more the Bible uses questions rather that statements . . . because a question is self-involving.
2. The use of parables.
3. The use of visual aids
4. The use of street theatre
5. The use of people (and their names) as living signs.[69]

Guinness explains:

> Apologetics is not primarily human, it is divine, God is the one who is doing it – we only come under him, at best. It is not primary defensive,

---

[69] O.S Guinness. *A Biblical Basis for Apologetics*. https://www.bethinking.org/apologetics/the-essence-of-apologetics/2-biblical-basis (Accessed July 12, 2017)

it's primarily prosecution. It is not solely intellectual — it is intellectual — come — moral — come spiritual. It is not a matter of answering people's questions; it's not even purely literal or verbal. In the Old Testament it's dramatic and uses the whole of life as means. . . .It's not just one to one or purely individual; it's also used nationally and corporately. . . .But all of it rooted in this idea of God being framed in the dock and therefore faith wants to clear God, so concerned is it with the zeal for this name and His character.[70]

Apologetics in the New Testament

The establishment of the New Testament church ushered in new breed of heresies and criticisms. The availability of writing materials and the rise of professional scribes also made it possible for writings to be copied rapidly and economically. Thus these heretics were able to make their voice heard widely. Some of these heretics include Hymenaeus and Philetus which Apostle Paul mentioned in his epistle to Timothy (2Tim.2:17).

These heretics became increasingly uncomfortable with the New Testament doctrines related to man's

---

[70] Ibid

sin, total depravity, salvation by grace through faith alone, etc., because these New Testament teachings were in contrast with their perverted teachings. All the unique Bible passages received clearer explanation and exposition in New Testament and this in turn made a lot of the heretics uncomfortable. As long as the divine message was partly veiled, these critics did not worry much. The apostolic teachings of the first century clearly exposed their errors, biases, and prejudices. No longer could they maintain their brand of theology, seeing that now the fundamental tenets of biblical theology were spelled out clearly.

In the Gospels

There were several apologetic activities present in the gospels. Matthew started his writing by defending the Davidic origin of the Messiah. Furthermore, phrases like, "so that it may be fulfilled. . ." found across the gospel of Matthew is to convince the Jews of Jesus' day that the coming of Jesus is the fulfillment of the Messianic prophecies recorded in the Prophets.

The documentation of His miracles in the gospels was also meant to defend the Messiahship of Jesus. Luke gave an orderly account of the life and works of Jesus and also presented the claims that Jesus is the Messiah. Also, in the gospel of John, the evangelist presented Jesus in His divinity, as one who was with the Father from the beginning and also makes strong emphasis on the humanity of Christ also. According to John, seeing Jesus is seeing God. John defended this by recording the miracles of Jesus and ultimately the resurrection of Jesus from the dead which is the greatest attestation to His divinity.

In Acts

The Apostle Peter's speech at Pentecost was apologetic. Also Stephen, before his martyrdom attempted to defend his truth claims and Apostle Paul, during his trials made various defense for his faith. A significant portion of Paul's epistles were also apologetic in nature. One of the pivotal passages for Christian apologetics is found in Acts 17:16-33, where Paul reasoned with the Jews, the God-fearing gentiles, the Epicurean and Stoic philosophers. Also in Acts 18:24-28, Apollos, a man well-versed in the scriptures and an eloquent speaker refuted the Jews vigorously in public debate, demonstrating from the scriptures that Jesus was the Christ. Writing from prison in Philippians 1:16, Paul the Apostle speaks of himself as sent there 'for the defense of the gospel'. Bruce reveals:

> The Epistle to the Romans, however, is written to Christians; in his indictment of paganism in its opening chapter Paul is preaching to the converted. There are two passages in Acts where the gospel is shown in direct confrontation with paganism, and these two passages anticipate the main line of second-century Christian apologetic against the pagans. They are the passages which record Barnabas and Paul's protest against idolatry at Lystra (Acts 14:8-18), and Paul's address before the court of the Areopagus at Athens (Acts 17:16-34). The gospel confronted unsophisticated pagans in the former place, sophisticated pagans in the latter.[71]

In The Epistles

There were Jews who created problems in Galatia, Ephesus, and other places. The epistle to the Galatians was a refutation of the wrong doctrines

---
[71] Bruce, Ibid., 35-36

present among the Galatians. There were Gnostics who tried to amalgamate Christian theology with occult philosophies. The Epistle to Colossians is an apologetics against them. The epistle to Hebrews is an apologetics against another heresy and the Acts of the Apostles is another relevant apologetic and polemic book in the New Testament. Jude had to remind his readers to contend for the faith against those who would want to distort the Christian message. Apologetic and polemical activities were common and strong in the church

Peter warned his readers against those who mocked at statements in portions of the New Testament, and so on. Scoffers and critics raised several objections against the Christian faith and they made attempts to distort the biblical truths. Instead of ignoring them, the New Testament writers wrote extensively to expose their erroneous objections, condemned them, and also established the truth.

Having studied the New Testament's apologetic activities, Guinness came up with the following conclusions from the New Testament evidences:

1. Apologetics is biblical, not post-biblical
2. It has nothing to do, with 'being apologetic'
3. The New Testament metaphors are mainly legal, not military
4. Apologetics covers the formal and informal defense
5. It is for all Christians, not just for some
6. It is used with 'insider' as well as 'outsiders'
7. It is profoundly intellectual, but it is equally powerful morally and spiritually.[72]

---

[72]Guinness, Ibid

CHAPTER FOUR

Brief History of Christian Apologetics

Discussing the historical origin of Christian apologetics and polemics is very pertinent. Even our Christian faith has its clarity in history and Christianity itself is a historical religion, which cannot exist apart from the Jesus of history.

The Christian faith is solidly and inseparably rooted in history. If the accounts of creation, Adam, Eve, Eden, the flood, Moses, the exodus of the Jews, the prophets, Jesus, the crucifixion, resurrection, ascension of Jesus, Pentecost, and the apostles are eliminated from the Bible, then nothing substantial remains of the Christian faith. Ultimately, all the foundational, cardinal, and the essential doctrines of Christianity depends on the historicity of the events recorded in the Bible. If studying of history have such importance to the Christian faith, then discussing its historical origin is equally important.

Christianity has always faced serious political and ecclesiastical attacks right from its inception and pagan intellectuals have not ceased in their attempts to file up criticism against the Bible, the deity of Christ and the Christian faith at large. As Christianity spread through the Roman Empire, Philosophers and intellectuals raised fierce attacks on the Christian faith and Christianity, without any sense of courtesy and they branded Christianity as an absurd religion. Pliny the younger called Christianity a "contagious superstition" in his letter to Emperor Trojan.[73]

The charges filed up against the early Church, which led to their massive persecutions were the emphases of Christ's supremacy and preference over Caesar, teachings about salvation by grace through faith and not as the result of keeping the laws, insurrection, cannibalism, secrecy, etc. Another reason for the rise of critics, heretics and heretical movements was the New Testaments itself. The New Testament

---

[73] Ibid., 39

doctrines related to man's sin, total depravity, the deity of Jesus, salvation by grace through faith alone, etc. made the opponents of Christianity uncomfortable and this led to the persecution of the church and the rise of many heretical teachings in the church, which called for the urgent response of the early apologists and polemicists.

Apologetic and polemical activities were common and strong in the church from the first to the fifth century of the early church but unfortunately became inactive for almost a thousand years. The iconoclasm of the early Christians and the Christian faith necessitated the need for the first century Apostles and the church fathers to make defense for the faith both in voice and pen.[74] Though Apologetics was purely a New Testament activity, yet, in the Old Testament, various attempts were made by the prophets to defend the God of Israel as the only God who is capable of true justice and powerful to save and

---

[74]Johnson C. Philip and Saneesh Cherian, *Introduction to Integrated Christian Apologetics* (India: A Calvin Research Group Academic Resource, 2003), 4

do the impossible. Example of this can be traced to the encounter of Elijah with the prophets of Baal, some parts of Job, Psalm 19; 24, etc. all have apologetic appeals in them.[75]

Also in the New Testament, right from the birth of the church, the church had engaged herself in various apologetic activities. Apostle Peter at Pentecost had to make an extemporaneous apologetic speech to establish that the experience of the 120 on the day of Pentecost was the fulfillment of Jehovah's prophecy in Joel 2:28, rather than a mere acrobatic display resulting from drunkenness. Deacon Stephen before his martyrdom defended his truth claims and the Apostle Paul, during his trial made various defense for his faith.

During the second and third centuries great apologists and polemicists emerged and made several attempts to convince the Roman states and the skeptics that the Christians had done nothing to deserve such persecutions inflicted upon them. The

---

[75] Philip and Cherian, *Introduction to Integrated Christian Apologetics*, 5

likes of Justin martyr and Iranaeus did a great job in this respect. From the beginning of the church down to this present day, countless Christian apologists and polemicists have emerged to defend the Christian faith through voice and pen. Bruce has this to say: "The second century AD is the period specially known as 'the age of the apologists'. It was the age when Christian leaders began to fight back against the repressive policy of the Roman state, regarding the pen as a mightier and worthier weapon than the sword".[76]

To mention but a few, men like Theophilus of Antioch, Tertullian, St. Augustine, Minicius Felix, Justin Martyr, Anselm, Thomas Aquinas, Quadratus, Aristides, C.S. Lewis, Basil Mitchell, Bernard L. Ramm, Paul E. Little, Matt Slick, Norman L. Geisler, Josh McDowell, Van Til, C.H Pinnock, Lee Strobel, Ravi Zacharias, Cheung Vincent, Johnson C. Philip, Saneesh Cherians, etc. had contributed immensely to the field of Christian Apologetics.

---

[76] Bruce, vii

Early African Apologists

The history of Christian apologetics will be incomplete without mentioning the immense contributions of some notable African Christian fathers to Christian apologetics. Great teachers, leaders, and apologists came from Africa. These include Tertullian, Origen, Cyprian, Clement of Alexandria, Augustine and others. They defended the Christian faith through their writings and teachings.

To mention but a few, Athanasius of Alexandria, a noted Egyptian leader of the fourth century, is remembered for his affirmation of the Trinity. Also Augustine of Hippo, known for his book titled the "The City of God," in which he defended Christianity from pagan critics. He was born in present-day Algeria, educated in North Africa and he was known for his indelible contribution to Christianity. Augustine opposed heresies, such as Pelagianism—A Christian belief that denies the view of original sin and the necessity of grace, asserting that man is capable of achieving salvation by his own efforts. Tertullian was also a prolific writer of apologetic, theological and controversial works. He was born in Carthage, an ancient city in North Africa, in modern Tunisia.

Although, like every other church fathers, some of these African fathers erred at some points, but their contributions to Christianity cannot be denied.

CHAPTER FIVE

Purpose and Values of Christian Apologetics

It is essential to note that apologetics is not for proving the word of God; neither is it meant to make the Bible become truthful by making logical defense for it as though it is a helpless book. Apologetics is not to render a helping hand to the scriptures but simply to provide a basis for faith and help the sincere inquirer. Bernard Ramm summarizes the purpose of Christian apologetics into three reasonable points:

1. To show how the Christian faith is related to truth claims.

2. To show Christian's power of interpretation.

3. Christian apologetics is that of refutation.[77]

In addition, the values of Christian apologetics can also be summarized with the follow sentences:

1. Becoming a more complete person

---

[77] Bernard L. Ramm, *A Christian Appeal to Reason* (Irving, Texas: International Correspondence Institute, 1968), 15

2. Knowing what to use and what not to use in public presentations.
3. Prevention against future assaults of the enemy.

Bruce also maintains, ". . . in every form of Christian witness, including apologetic and polemic, the object must always to be to commend the Savior to others. A Victory in debate is a barren thing compared with the winning of men and women to the cause of Christ".[78]

Calvin Research Group gives more satisfying lists of the purpose of Apologetics which are listed and explained below:

1. **Apologetics is a Man-ward Operation.** The primary purpose of Christian apologetics is to expose errors, refute the error and establish the truth. It therefore attempts to make a reasonable and constructive defense for the reliability of the scriptures and its claims as the only inspired word of God which is the only unique factor that distinguishes the Bible from other literature and legendries. Apologetics makes a

---

[78] Bruce, *First-Century Faith*, viii

defense not to approve the Bible as truth.[79] The Bible needs no human approval to declare it true. Apologists themselves have no say of their own apart from what the Bible says and established. Therefore, Christian Apologetics is a man-ward operation in that, its activity is not directed towards the Bible itself.

According to Calvin research group, the purpose of Christian Apologetics is not to defend the Bible with the attitude as though it is a helpless book. Rather, it is a man-ward operation meant to help those who are perplexed or distressed due to doubts.[80] Therefore, the defense of the Bible is presented not for preserving the scriptures but to preserve the faith of the inquirer. This is what is meant by man-ward operation.

2. **Apologetics Has Limits.** Since apologetics is a man-ward operation, it can never be used to prove that the Bible is the word of God. The best that it can do in this matter is to point to the unusual character of the Bible in matters of unity, accuracy, consistency, historicity

---

[79] Philip and Cherian, *Introduction to Integrated Christian Apologetics*, 11

[80] Ibid

and life-changing power.⁸¹ The rest is left to the inquirer. Accepting the Bible as God's word comes only by an act of faith in which apologetics can only play a supportive role. Thus the purpose of apologetics is neither to establish the Bible as God's word, nor to create faith in skeptical minds. Rather, its purpose is to aid a person to see that the attacks brought up against the bible are NOT valid. Once it is demonstrated that statements of the Bible and the facts of science do not conflict with each other, the way is cleared for the sincere inquirer for making the leap of faith.⁸²

Apologists does not provide or claim to have total verification or factual substantiation of all issues recorded in the scriptures. His concern should only rest upon the question: is there enough factual and reliable support from the study of ancient history, archaeology, science and geography to affirm that the Bible is true in its claims? Therefore, the task of the apologist is not to present total verification of all

---

[81] Ibid

[82] Ibid

things because not all history has been recorded, and not even all recorded history has been preserved. Some statements about geographical matters in scripture are still obscure; though this does not deny the existence of such.[83]

3. **Barrier Removal is the Prime Target.** By barrier, the researcher means any fence or gate — either it is intellectual, social, psychological or spiritual — that prevents one in moving in a particular direction. Apologetics therefore seeks to help sincere inquirers to remove every barrier that hinders their faith.[84] The barriers might be intellectual barrier, social barrier, psychological barrier or spiritual barrier that often militates against the ability of the inquirers to accept the gospel with faith and simplicity of mind. This may hinder believers in Christ of their access to the deeper understanding of the truth.

Apologetics therefore centers its tasks not only on creation of faith in the inquirer, because this can only

---

[83] Afolabi, *Defending What You Believe*, 53

[84] Philip & Cherian, *Introduction to Integrated Christian Apologetics*, 12

play a little supportive role, but its major concern is the removal of barriers which will later build up the faith of unbelieving inquirers and also helps believers in Christ to be deeper in their commitments to Christ.

4. **Rationalist Demands Might be a Boon.** Our rationalist age places many demands before a statement is accepted as true. Many people think that this rationalism is sure to destroy the Bible. On the contrary, this is a blessing in disguise. Many demands placed by the rational thinkers give us excellent standards with which to evaluate our statements objectively.[85]

Enough information and evidences exist today to show, using the more sound principles of rational thinking, that the Bible is a unique book. However, no amount of evidence can force a person claiming to be a rationalist against his will to believe even though the rational content of Christianity is fully logical, accurate, and reliable. Christian Apologetics is not meant for these people. Apologetics is meant for those

---

[85] Ibid

sincere seekers who want to know how reliable the rational content of the Bible is.[86]

5. **Apologetics Demands Willing Reception.** Apologists should be aware that the task or the purpose of Christian Apologetics is not to impose a belief or any idea into the minds of deliberate skeptics who have deliberately decided not to accept the Christian faith or believe its truth claims. Apologetics is not the treatment or antidote for willful unbelief, neither is it meant to coax anyone who had developed a strong personal antipathy towards the Christian faith to believe. Rather, it is meant to serve as a cure for sincere doubts with the continuous use of the word of God and dependence on the Holy Spirit's intervention.[87]

6. **Apologetics in not Scientism.** Many thoughtless scientists had wrongly believed that everything has to be empirically explained before it is considered true. Therefore, the apologist recognizes that his aim is not

---

[86] Ibid

[87] Ibid

to explain everything with the help of science.[88] Rather, he uses science where it is a scientific subject, history where it is a historical subject, logic where it is a logical subject, and so on. He also recognizes that in some places none of these subjects applies, but that the subject can be understood only with faith. In such places he emphasis faith.[89]

In summary, the main and important task of apologetics is the verification of truth claims. The question is, how can one verify the truthfulness of a statement or an idea? Edward Carnell lists several criteria available to judge the truthfulness of a statement or idea.

1. **Instinct**: Instinct is a natural tendency or ability to behave or react in a particular way without having to learn it or think about it (Longman Dictionary of Contemporary English). According of Carnell, judging by instinct is the lowest level of judgment. He maintains: "There is an instinctive belief in the

---

[88] Ibid

[89] Ibid., 13

supernatural and in life after death, an impulse to worship, an awareness of guilt—all common to men. Although instinct may be a pointer toward truth, it lacks adequacy as a test for truth, since it is not possible to determine clearly what is purely instinctive and what the product of environmental conditioning is."[90] Undeniably, instinct is real but it is a subjective reality. Therefore, it is not adequate enough to verify truth.[91]

2. **Custom:** Custom is an established, socially accepted practice known of a group of people. It influences the behaviour of the people and their belief systems. Because of its influence on a group of people who have adopted such custom and habitually practiced it, it therefore carry a special kind of authority in the community such custom is practiced and its hold on the particular group cannot be easily broken. However, employing custom as a tool for verifying truth is

---

[90] Ibid

[91] Edward John Carnell, *An Introduction to Christian Apologetics* (Grand Rapids; MI: Eerdmans, 1948).

inadequate because a custom may be good or bad, pleasant to some and unpleasant to other groups of people outside the practicing custom.[92]

3. **Consensus Gentium:** It is from a Latin word meaning the agreement of the people. It is an ancient criterion for truth. The consensus Gentium states that, "That which is universal among men carries the weight of truth". It is also referred to as the climate of opinion, community sentiment, general belief, conventional wisdom, prevailing sentiment, etc. One might conclude in his mind that a universally accepted belief must be an assurance that it is undeniably true.[93]

However, various scientific discoveries had shown that many prevailing sentiments and beliefs accepted universally were not actually true. For example, in the early stages of computer programming people thought that pure mathematical computation could produce "artificial intelligence". After about half a century of

---

[92] Afolabi, *Defending What You Believe*, 57

[93] Ibid

working with computers every computer expert today knows that this presupposition was totally wrong. Therefore, conventional wisdom can err.[94] This is not, therefore, a reliable test for truth.

4. **Feeling:** the usage of the word "feeling" as used in the field of psychology differs in meaning and varies in application. Feeling may refer to coetaneous sensation, especially the sense of touch. But in relation to this discussion, feeling means an inward impression or perception one may have, which may later amount to a genuine conviction. Although no one can deny its reality but it is a subjective reality.[95] Carnell maintains that, "Without inwardness, religion is sterile and barren. But, as a test for truth, intuition and subjective feeling may mislead a person. Feelings and intuitions themselves must be subjected to some other standard of truth."[96]

---

[94] Ibid

[95] Ibid., 57

[96] Ibid

5. **Sense Perception:** it is certain that most, if not all, of our knowledge of the world comes from sensation and we are able to relate with our environment through a variety of sensory modalities which we possess. Aristotle distinguished five senses: vision, hearing, touch, taste, and smell. Of a truth, we all tend to believe what we can visually behold and argue for its reality.

However, the legitimacy of the evidences that our senses provides is still subject to debate by various philosophers. For example, our perception of taste and smell is relative and even what we claim to see may actually not be what the object truly represents. Sense perception is indeed a valid source of truth, but still, our senses may occasionally deceive us. Therefore, sense perception is not adequate in itself as a final test for truth verification.[97]

6. **Pragmatism:** the theory of pragmatism holds that the test of truth is to be found in its practical consequences. If the practical consequences are

---

[97] Ibid., 29

satisfactory, the idea is said to be true. This statement is true to some extent but the limitation of this theory is that it does not establish what is true but what works. Lying may bring satisfactory consequences but that does not make it true.[98] Carnell concludes, "In everyday experience as finite beings, we do not possess sufficient insight and understanding to know if the ultimate consequences of a given course of action will prove beneficial or destructive. Our limited vision of consequences diminishes the worth of pragmatism as a test for truth".[99]

7. **Consistency:** Many scholars actually settled for a consistency test as the most reliable tool for verifying truth. Truth is not self-contradictory and vague. It is verifiable and must be consistent with reality. Consistency test brings an idea or any given paradigm into judgment to see if its claims have any measure of trustworthiness, constancy and agreement with any

---

[98] Ibid., 30

[99] Ibid

presentable evidence.[100] However, Carnell maintains that there is a limitation to consistency as a test for truth because some untrue notions may not be self-contradictory. Nevertheless, according to Carnell, in spite of its limitation, consistency is one pointer in the direction of truth.

8. **Coherence:** coherence is the situation in which all the parts of something fit together well. According to Carnell, coherence goes beyond consistency. It is the combination of self-consistency and a comprehensive view of all experience. This is what Carnell refers to a "systematic consistency". By this he means that which horizontally is self-consistent (non-contradictory) and vertically fits the facts of experience.[101]

---

[100] Ibid

[101] Ibid

CHAPTER SIX

Branches of Christian Apologetics

Christian Apologetics is not a one sided or narrow subject dealing with Bible and science alone, but is a vast subject with several branches dealing with various opposing views against the Christian faith. Increase in knowledge in the recent centuries had exposed the Christian faith to a more fierce opposition and new provoking questions attempted to relegate the scriptures had equally been directed to the Christian faith and the Bible. Consequently, the task of Christian Apologetics also keeps widening, with new topics coming into prominence as the opponents of the Christian faith also continue to present an ever-widening array of questions against the Bible and the Christian faith.[102] The branches of apologetics are as follows:

---

[102] Ibid., 59

1. **Biblical apologetics:** Biblical apologetics include issues concerned with the authorship and date of biblical books, biblical canon and biblical inerrancy.[103]

2. **Philosophical Apologetics:** Philosophical apologetics concerns itself primarily with the arguments for the existence of God, although they do not exclusively focus on this area. They do not argue for the veracity of Christianity over other religions but merely for the existence of a Creator deity.[104]

3. **Rational Apologetics:** Rational apologetics address diverse subjects; e.g., Bible difficulties, Bible and science, Bible and evolution, Bible and astronomy, and cosmology. The rise of the Theory of Evolution in the nineteenth century has resulted in the development of creationism as a part of rational apologetics. Today, Creationism is one of the most advanced areas in Rational Apologetics.[105]

---

[103] Adeogun, Ibid. 22.

[104] Ibid.

[105] Afolabi, *Defending What You Believe*, 64

4. **Classical Apologetics.** *Classical apologetics* is so called because it was the apologetic method practiced by the first thinkers who studied and practiced the application of reason to the defense of Christianity. These pioneer apologists included Augustine, Anselm, and Thomas Aquinas . . . The roots of classical apologetics are found in some second and third century apologists as well. Classical apologetics stresses rational arguments for the existence of God and historical evidence supporting the truth of Christianity. Stress is placed on miracles as a confirmation of the claims of Christ and the biblical prophets and apostles.[106]

5. **Evidential Apologetics**: Evidential apologetics stresses the need for evidence in support of the Christian truth claims. The evidence can be rational, historical, archaeological, and even experiential. Since it is so broad, it understandably overlaps with other types of apologetics.[107]

---

[106] Norman Geisler, *Baker Encyclopedia of Christian Apologetics* (Grand Rapids: Baker Books, 1999), 79.

[107] Ibid

6. **Presuppositional Apologetics**: Presuppositional apologetics affirms that one must defend Christianity from the foundation of certain basic presuppositions. Usually, a presuppositionalist presupposes the basic truth of Christianity and then proceeds to show (in any of several ways) that Christianity alone is true.[108]

---

[108] Ibid., 81-82

CHAPTER SEVEN

Presuppositions of Christian Apologetics

Presuppositions are the starting assumptions upon which the rest of the subjects are built. Though some presuppositions are axiomatic (self-proven) in nature, and they need no further proofs. For example, one plus one will automatically give you two. No further proof in needed for establishing axiomatic presuppositions. However, opposing presuppositions will have to be analyzed, tested, or shown to be false to prove or disprove their veracity. Our most basic presuppositions about reality therefore form the foundation of our world view and greatly influence the way we think and perceive things. Vincent Cheung declares:

> Our presuppositions determine our interpretation of what we observe, so that we can observe exactly the same things and come up with different conclusions. Although I would say that non-Christian presuppositions cannot even support non-

Christian conclusions, neither can they be used to support for Christianity, for the reason that non-Christian presuppositions really cannot support anything.[109]

Understanding and carefully analyzing the presupposition of others will give the apologist the ability to expose the fallacy of the claims of others and refute every presupposition that steamed out of false assumptions of randomness and blind chance. When such erroneous presuppositions are exposed, the opposing parties lose ground and inevitably bow for the truth.

Major presuppositions of some prominent Christian groups

1. **Fundamentalists** (Theological Conservatives): Fundamentalist as a term for expression refers to a person who holds or upholds a strict or literal interpretation of traditional religious beliefs. They strictly uphold the basic or essential doctrines of their religious beliefs. Fundamentalists are also known as

---

[109] Vincent Cheung, *Presuppositional Confrontations* (USA: Reformation Ministries International, 2003), 12

the conservatives or the orthodox. "Orthodox" here is used in a theological sense, rather than as a denominational title such as Eastern Orthodox.[110]

Fundamental Christian Presuppositions are:

i. Sola Scriptura: The fundamental Christians believe that the Bible is the Holy Spirit-inspired word of God, and is the source of all revelation, doctrine, and authority. They give no attention to any other documents like the Apocrypha books as the inspired word of God.

ii. Sola Gratia: Grace alone is the basis of salvation. In reference to the Apostle Paul's assertion in Ephesians 2 vs. 8-9, fundamental Christians maintain that man is incapable of saving himself or obtaining salvation; it is purely on the basis of God's unmerited favor (Grace) that is lavished on sinners.

iii. Sola Fidei: Fundamental Christians holds that faith in the redemptive work of Christ is the only means through which one can attain gift justification. Faith is a non-meritorious activity.

---

[110] Afolabi, *Defending What You Believe*, 73

iv. Solus Christus: This presupposition holds that Christ is the only Savior and the mediator between God and man. There is no other savior or mediator. According to the doctrines of fundamentalist Christianity, anyone who denies any of the above tenets is considered heretic.[111]

2. **Evangelicals:** The word evangelical was actually a synonym for fundamentalist. Today "Evangelical" implies a more liberal view. In the original sense, an Evangelical is a doctrinally conservative Christians who belief that salvation is through Jesus alone. Evangelicals stress both doctrinal absolutes and vigorous efforts to win others to belief. Evangelical Christians also believe in Sola Scriptura (Scripture alone), Sola Gratia (Grace alone), Sola Fide (Faith alone), and Solus Christus (Christ alone).[112]

3. **Neo-evangelicals:** A new group emerged in the middle of nineteen century who wanted to be identified with the "evangelicals" but were not willing to accept

---

[111] Ibid

[112] Ibid

the accuracy and the reliability of the biblical narratives.

Neo Evangelical Presuppositions are:

i. A somewhat fallible bible

ii. Probable Theistic Evolution

iii. Probability of salvation without an explicit knowledge of Christ

iv. Doubt about veracity of miracles recorded in the Bible.

v. They deny that the scripture is complete through their attempts to Christianize pagan ideas and systems founded upon personal beliefs and or influences such as psychology/psychiatry.[113]

4. **Radicals** (Wrongly Termed LIBERALS): There are basically two forms of radicals: Christian radicals and the extreme radicals. However, the Christian radicals are also divided into two distinct forms, namely, liberals and extreme radicals. The liberals totally and completely reject the orthodox or conservative position of structured religious organizations. These Christians

---

[113] Johnson C. Philip, *Branches of Apologetics* (India: A Calvin Research Group Academic Resource, 2003), 5

are radicals of one form or another and tend to lean towards the liberalism as seen in modern churches and their acceptances of same sex couples, homosexual priests, and bishops, and modern written Bibles that are less restrictive.[114]

Radical Presuppositions are:

i. A rejection of all tenets of conservative Christianity

ii. All religions eventually lead to salvation

iii. Everyone will eventually attain heaven

iv. The Bible is not the sole word of God

v. The Bible contains plenty of errors and primitive ideas

vi. The record of creation is a myth, while Evolution is fact

vii. Virgin birth, resurrection of Christ, and miracles are myths.[115]

5. **Christian Mystics:** Christian mystics seek one or mere mystical encounters for spiritual joy and assurance. Christian mystics are found both among

---

[114] Ibid

[115] Ibid

Roman Catholics and Protestants. They are concerned about a spiritual transformation of the human person to achieve full realization of their human potential, which was realized most perfectly in Jesus and is manifested in others though their association with Him. They are not to be confused with Christian spiritism as many do.

Christian Mystic presuppositions are:

i. Rejection of Bible alone

ii. Rejection of doctrine and theology

iii. Elevation of mystical experience to the Level of Revelation

iv. Salvation through mystical experience

v. Spiritual joy through mystical experience.[116]

6. **Christian Cults**: The term 'Christian cult' sounds quite oxymoronic. One would ask what Christianity has to do with cultism or how does cultism find its way into Christianity. Josh McDowell defines a cult as "A perversion, a distortion of biblical Christianity, and as

---

[116] Ibid., 8

such, rejects the historic teachings of the Christian Church".[117]

The presuppositions of Christian cults are as follows:

i. Rejection of Sola Scriptura and Elevation of their own books to the level of the Bible.

ii. Rejection of salvation by grace through faith

iii. Rejecting the uniqueness and the divinity of Jesus Christ

iv. Rejection of normal hermeneutics

v. Claim that only they are true Children of God

vi. Rejection of one or more of the biblical doctrines related to sin, salvation, grace, justification, hell, etc.[118] The following Christian groups are categorized under Christian cults: The church of Jesus Christ of the Latter Day Saints (Mormons), Jehovah's Witnesses, Church Universal and Triumphant, Moonies: Unification of Christianity, Holy order of MANS, Central London Church of Christ, Eckancar, and Church of the living God to mention but a few.

---

[117] Josh McDowell, *A Ready Defense* (Nashville: Thomas Nelson Publishers, 1993), 332

[118] Philip, Ibid., 9

CHAPTER EIGHT

Current Challenges in African Christianity

Since its inception, Christianity in Africa has grown exponentially. However, its growth has given room to inconsistencies and doctrinal discrepancies among the professing Christians. There seems to be different versions of Christianity existing in Africa today, which are totally different in forms and practices from what was initially passed on by the pioneering missionaries.

Consequent to the doctrinal disparities which exist among Christians in Africa, skeptics have questioned the integrity of the Christian faith, its doctrines, and ultimately the person of Jesus. Furthermore, religious syncretism has become the major part of Christianity in Africa and this need to be given critical attention.

Syncretism and its Modern Trend in Africa

The English word "syncretism" comes from the Greek word *synkretismos*. Its origin is the custom of the people who lived in the Island of Crete in ancient days, who always fought themselves, but when enemies from outside attacked, they combined force with each other to combat their foreign enemy. They called this practice synkretismos, which comes from the verb meaning 'to combine'. The concept is also employed to refer to the uniting of quarreling brothers in the face of common enemies. Generally, syncretism would refer to the attempt to unite together those elements which do not agree.[119]

There is virtually no religion that is totally free from syncretism. All religions possess some level of syncretism. Islam for example, was originally influence by Arab culture. Christianity draws heavily from Judaism and the Jewish culture. Some icons and symbols used in Christianity did not originate from

---

[119] Elizabeth Ezenweke & Ikechukwu Kanu, *Perspectives of Syncretism and Its Modern Trend: A Case of Christian and African Traditions*. http://dx.doi.org/10.4314/ujah.v13i2.4 (accessed November 8, 2018).

Christianity. The crucifix, which later became the most used symbol in Christianity, was adopted from the Roman culture. This makes total removal of syncretic elements from religion like Christianity a difficult task, because Christianity exists without a cultural environment and Africa Christianity is pervaded by indigenous influences.

Some African scholars have called for the abolition of the word 'syncretism' and suggest that a more constructive word like enculturation should be used to replace it. In its true sense, syncretism occurs in Christianity when the basic elements of the gospel are replaced by religious elements from the host culture or other cultures. It gives room for the amalgamation of other religious elements with Christianity. It brings Christianity into a synthesis with something totally alien to it. This is quite different from enculturation. Crollius explained enculturation in this manner:

> Enculturation means the honest and serious attempt to make Christ and his Gospel of salvation ever more understood by people of every culture, locality and time. It is the reformulation of Christian life and doctrine into the very thought patterns of each other. . . .It is

the continuous endeavor to make Christianity 'truly feel at home' in the cultures of each people.[120]

Unfortunately, most churches in Africa have not been able to differential between inculturation, enculturation and syncretism. Some cultural beliefs and practices which are antithetical to the Christian faith have been inserted into Christianity, and these are expressed in prayers, liturgies and songs. For example, speaking to one's offering in the church, and phrases like, "speak to your offering what you want it to bring back to you" are practices found in some African religions, and these practices were brought into Christianity.

Examples of these syncretic practices abound: asking for soap and sponge, broom, candles, cocoanut, cutlass and the like to be brought to church for prayers fall into this category. In some Christian denominations in Africa, church members were asked to bring live rams, pigeons, and the like for their

---

[120] R. A Crollius, *Inculturation: Newness and ongoing progress*. In J. Walligo (Ed.). *Making a church that is truly African in inculturation: Its meaning and urgency* (Nairobi: Pauline, 1986), 11

'redemption'. Some were asked to give money, foodstuff, salt, used dresses and other domestic items to beggars on the street, not for any humanitarian service, but to either avert impending danger, win the goodwill of some spiritual entities, attract the sympathy of one's ancestors or to win some sorts of favor. The dangers in these practices are enormous. It beclouds 'innocent' believers from trusting solely in the redemptive work of Christ and they see these things as complements to the atoning work of Christ.

One disgusting example is of a pastor in the eastern part of Nigeria who called his congregation for warfare prayers against their enemies and asked them to come along with a cutlass each to butcher their spiritual enemies (although, this is more of ignorance than syncretism). Another example is of a pastor who asked a man who came to him for prayer to visit the burial site of the founder of his denomination and make his requests known to God there. These practices are grossly foreign to biblical Christianity. Ezenweke and Kanu also pointed out some forms of modern day syncretism in the African church. They stated:

Another form of modern day syncretism in the church is usually nurtured and propagated during interreligious dialogues. Because the world is becoming one politically, technically and economically there is a felt need to be drawn together in a universal brotherhood. Religions are also called upon to unit with one another. Christians, Muslims, and African Traditional Religion (ATR) are told to find common beliefs to unite them, and in many cases, this places a political pressure upon Christian churches, and the end result is syncretism and the compromise of the gospel. Here, the quality and compatibility of religions are justified by subsuming their various categories under generic categories. For instance, we speak of the different deities of the different religions as "transcendent". We say we serve the same God.[121]

Like I said earlier, total removal of all syncretic elements from religion like Christianity may be impossible, but any practice or ideology which may lead to the reinterpretation or misrepresentation of biblical Christianity must be discouraged. Put succinctly, the point at which syncretism becomes a menace to Christianity is when it maligns the

---

[121] Ezenkwere & Kanu, Ibid

redemptive work of Christ or causes the misrepresentation of the Christian faith, and when this is not condemned in the church, Christianity will be robbed of its purity, the gospel message will be compromised, and the Bible may cease to be the final authority in the matters of faith and Christian practice among Africans.

CHAPTER NINE

The Concept of God in ATR, Islam and Christianity

African Traditional Religion or better called *African Religions*, Islam and Christianity are the three basic religions in Africa and they all have something important to tell us about God.

God in African Religions

Although, African religions do not have known founders or sacred books we can draw references from, rituals and oral narratives are the main materials from which we can derive the beliefs of African people about God from. Africans do not have any problem believing in the existence of God, and they are not strangers to the worship of One True God—Supreme Being, the creator of the universe. Africans' belief in the Supreme Being called "God" is revealed in their references to Him as the living eternal being, the creator of all things, one who is ageless, all-knowing, all-powerful, and omnipresent.

Similar to the biblical attributes of God, Africans believe that God, whom they call by different names, is perfect in all His ways, holy, just, loving, caring, imperishable, infinite and limitless in every respect. John S. Mbiti explains that though the knowledge of God as the Supreme Being is not documented in any sacred book, yet is "expressed in proverbs, short statements, songs, prayers, names, myths, stories and religious ceremonies".[122]

God is supreme and great over all visible and invisible beings or things that we believe to exist. One of the best Zulu names of God is 'Unkulunkulu', which means 'the Great-great-One' and like them the neighboring people call God as the 'Ndebele', which also means 'the Greatest of the great'. Like them, the Tonga, the Ngoni, the Akan, the Baluba and some

---

[122] John S. Mbiti, *African Religions and Philosophy* (London: Heinemann, 1969), 29

other tribes designate God as 'Great God', or Great One', or 'the Great King'.[123]

It is clear from the above discussion that the knowledge of God among Africans didn't originate from Christianity, Islam or any other oriental religions. This is why Mbiti said, "One should not, therefore, expect long dissertations about God. But God is no stranger to African peoples, and in traditional life there are no atheists".[124] Therefore, in African traditional ontology, God is seen and understood in the following ways:

1. God is Supreme. The belief in God, the Supreme Being, is widespread among Africans. By the supremacy of God, Africans see God as the one who is dominant, having power over all others. He is considered the greatest of all, the one who is situated as the highest point, without equal, without mate. The belief in God's supremacy affords Him the right to do whatever pleases Him. He depends on no one; He is

---

[123] *African Traditional Concept of God: A Critical Analysis.* Green University Review of Social Sciences, Vol.02, Issue 01, June 2015, pg. 3

[124] Mbiti, 29

self-reliant, self-sustaining, self-sufficient, and ultimately superior to all.

2. God is Transcendent and Immanent. In African traditional belief, God is both transcendent and immanent. As transcendent, God is uniquely other than everything in creation. God's being is eternal, the world's temporal. God's knowledge is total, human knowledge incomplete. God's character is holy, humanity's character fallen and sinful . . . God's energy is untiring and inexhaustible; the world's energy is subject to depletion through entropy. Hence, God is over and above persons in the world in all these respects.[125]

God has immanent features too and the idea of the immanence of God in Africans religions should not be seen from the pantheistic point of view. Africans see Him as God whose presence is felt by people within the natural world. For instance, the Yoruba tribe of Nigeria would express their beliefs in the nearness of God to His people through this moral advice: "Let he

---

[125]David Horton, *The Portable Seminary* (Michigan: Bethany House Publishers, 2006), 114

who perpetuate evil in the secret continue; if no man sees you, God is looking at you."

In African religions, God also demonstrates His immanence through intermediaries—minor deities, to whom the Supreme Being has delegated the supervisions of the affairs of the world and the people in it.

Mediation between God and humans is the chief religious role of the minor deities. They share this role with the ancestors, the elders, and the various religious functionaries of African societies. Harmony in the world and all the conditions for health, prosperity, and abundant life are achieved by the mediation of these multiple intermediaries. This conception of mediation is crucial for understanding the essence of African religions. Mediation is also one of the fundamental points of divergence between African religions and Christianity, since "the idea of intermediary divinities has no place in Christianity.[126]

3. God is Immortal and Eternal. The Yorubas often describe God as the *Oba aiku* (the ever-living King),

---

[126] Horton, *The Portable Seminary*, 405

Arugbo ojo (the ancient of days), *Olorun aiyeraiye* (the eternal God). In his review of the book of John S. Mbiti on *Concepts of God in Africa*, Bernard Ouma Onyango wrote:

> God is eternal, infinite and immutable. The Ngombe believe that the forest symbolizes agelessness and they use it metaphorically to praise God as "Bilikonda" the "Everlasting one of the Forest." The Ila and the Balube conceives God eternity and infinity in terms of the sun and addresses Him by the title Mutalabala which means eternal one. Just as the sun seems to be everlasting, so is God whose eternity is like a string or sum of many suns. The Tonga on the other hand calls God Tilo which means heaven, and they say in a proverb that, "heaven never dies; only men do!" This means that just as heaven is incapable of dying or destruction so is God who is eternal, infinite and immutable. The Gikuyu express the same concept when they say that God is the same today a He was yesterday and He is neither a child nor an old man. Likewise the Akan think of Him as eternal, infinite and the creator of the universe beyond who there is nothing, the supreme of the things of all that is being. The Yorubas also call Him the mighty immovable rock that never dies.

In a popular song they sing of Him that, "one never hears the death of God.[127]

God in Islamic Religion

Muslims, the follower of Islamic religion, believe in submitting to the one and only God, named *Allah.* Any deviation from this belief in one God or the belief that there is more than one person in God is idolatry and blasphemy called, *shirk.* This is why Muslims are opposed to the Christian doctrine of Trinity. One of the five pillars upon which Islam is built is the *SHAHĀDA* – bearing witness that there is no god but Allāh and that Muhammad is the Messenger of Allāh.

However, Muslims shared many doctrines with Christianity, such as creation, heaven, hell, angels, judgment and the resurrection of all people. Unfortunately, Islamic understanding of these doctrines does not always agree with the biblical teachings on them. The main focus of this discussion to examine what Muslim believes about God.

---

[127] Bernard Ouma Onyango, Book Review. John S. Mbiti: *Concepts of God in Africa,* http://pitti.over-blog.com/2018/12/johb-s.mbiti-concepts-of-god-in-africa.htm (accessed 13 September, 2019)

1. **God is the Absolute One**. Allah is described by Muslims in terms of several basic attributes. Fundamental to all is the attribute of absolute unity. Of all the Islamic God's attributes, the most important is his absolute and indivisible unity. To deny this is blasphemous. In sura 112, Muhammad defines God in these words: "Say: He is God, The One and Only; God, the Eternal, Absolute; He beggetteth not, Nor is He begotten; And there is none Like unto Him." This sura is held to be worth a third of the whole Qur'an; the seven heavens and the seven earths are founded upon it. Islamic tradition affirms that to confess this verse sheds one's sins "as a man might strip a tree in autumn of its leaves.[128] Assigning partners to God is the greatest sin in Islam and God will not forgive such sin (sura 4:116).

2. **God is the Absolute Ruler**. God is self-sustaining, self-existing, self-sufficient, the Knower of all that can be known, the controller and determiner of all things. Many of God's ninety-nine Islamic names speak of his sovereignty. He is:

---

[128] Horton, 395-6

- *Al-Adl*, the Just, whose word is perfect in veracity and Justice (6:115);
- *Al-Ali,* the High One, he who is high and might (2:225-26);
- *Al-Aziz*, the Sublime, mighty in his sublime sovereignty (59:23);
- *Al-Badi*, the Contriver, who contrived the whole art of creation (2:117);
- *Al-Hakim*, the Judge, who gives judgment among his servants(40:48-51);
- *Al-Hasib*, the Accounter, who is sufficient as a reckoner (4:6-7);
- *Al-Jabbar,* the Mighty One, whose might and power are absolute (59:23);
- *Al-Jalil*, the Majestic, mighty and majestic is he;
- *Al-Jami,* the Gatherer, who gathers all men to an appointed day (3:9);
- *Al-Malik*, the King, who is King of kings (59:23);
- *Al-Muizz*, the Honorer, who honors or abases who he will (3:26);
- *Al-Qadar,* the Able, who has the power to do what he pleases (17:99-101);

- *Al-Wakil*, the Administrator, who has charge of everything (6:102);
- *Malik al Mulk,* Possessor of the Kingdom, who grants sovereignty to whom he will (3:26).[129]

3. God as Absolute Justice. Several of God's names bespeak his absolute justice: the Majestic, the Gatherer, the Accounter, the Judge, the Just, the Most Holy One, to whom all in heaven and on earth ascribe holiness, the Observer of Justice, and the Avenger.[130]

4. Allah is a God of Love. The Qur'an teaches that Allah is a God of love and mercy. Sura 6:12 says He has imposed the law of mercy upon Himself. However, whether He loves all men is not so clear in Islam. Different Muslims interpret this subject in different ways, and not many Muslims will think of the love of God the way Christians do. The kind of love God demonstrated by giving His only Son, Jesus, even while we were yet sinners is a strange idea to most Muslims, but the Qur'an teaches about His love.

---

[129] Horton, 397-8

[130] Ibid

5. God as Absolute Will. There is certain mystery about God's names. Historian Kenneth Cragg affirms that these "are to be understood as characteristics of the divine will, rather than laws in his nature. Action that is arising from such descriptives, may be expected, but not as a matter of necessity." What gives unity to all God's actions is that he wills them all. As Willer he may be recognized by the descriptions given him, but he does not conform to any. The action of his will may be identified from its effects, but his will, of itself, is inscrutable. This accounts for the antithesis in certain God's names. For examples, God is "the One Who leads astray", as well as "the One Who guides."[131]

6. God is Absolutely Unknowable. Since everything is based in God's will and since his effects are sometimes contradictory and do not reflect any absolute essence, God's nature is utterly unknowable. . . .The attitude of God's absolute control over every aspect of his creation profoundly influences Islamic theology and culture.[132]

---

[131] Ibid

[132] Ibid

The Biblical Concept of God

The Bible does not make any attempt to define God, but presents descriptions of God as He has revealed Himself in His written word. We sometimes derive our knowledge of God through His names, His acts, His creation, statements credited to Him, and His activities in human history. However, fundamental to the nature of God are the truth that He is eternal, personal, spiritual, and holy.

1. God is Eternal. God is the uncreated Creator of the universe and mankind. He is self-existent and time places no limitation on Him. R.C. Sproul explains:

> Being eternal, God is not an effect. Since he is not an effect, he does not require a cause. He is uncaused. It is important to note the difference between an uncaused, self-existence eternal being and an effect that causes itself through self-creation.[133]

2. God is Personal. Over against any abstract neutral metaphysical concept, the God of Scripture is first and foremost a personal being. He reveals Himself by

---

[133] R.C. Sproul, *Reason to Believe* (Grand Rapids, Mich.: Zondervan, 1978), 112

names, especially the great personal name Yahweh, "I AM WHO I AM" (cf. Exodus 3:13-15; 6:3; Isaiah 42:8), and climatically in the person of Jesus, who is God in human flesh (John 1:14).[134] The centrality of God's personality is seen in that while He is the Creator and Preserver of all nature, He is encountered in Scripture not primarily as God of nature, as in pagan religions, but rather as the God of history, controlling and directing the affairs of humanity.[135] The personhood of God is more evident in His biblical description as Father.

God's personhood has been called into question on the basis of our use of the word *person* with respect to human beings. Human personhood involves limitation that allows relationship with another person or the world. To be a person means to be an individual among individuals. All of this cautions us against an erroneous anthropomorphizing of God. Biblically, it is more proper to see God's personhood as having priority

---

[134] Horton, 90

[135] Ibid

over that of man and therefore to understand human personhood theomorphously, i.e., a finite replica of the infinite divine person (cf. Genesis 1:26-27).[136]

The biblical concept of God's personhood refutes all abstract philosophical ideas of God as merely First Cause or Prime Mover as well as all naturalistic and pantheistic concepts.[137] It is reasonable to think of God in this light. Though He is spirit, yet He has all the elements of personality—will, intellect and feelings. He is not arbitrary; He acts according to His own will and purpose.

Furthermore, we know He created us in His own image and after His likeness. Since we are persons, God cannot possibly be anything less than a person. This does not suggest equality with Him in any form; He is absolutely distinct from all He created. His personhood is also expressed through His moral attributes—love and holiness. On the final note, because God is a Person, He is capable of relationship

---

[136] Ibid

[137] Ibid

with man; this makes communication between God and man possible.

3. God is Spirit. His personhood does not place any limitation on Him—He is all-wise, omnipotent, infinite, changeless and eternal. He is a spirit, meaning 'absolute power and life giver (Job 4:24). His spiritual nature prohibits any limitations on Him. He cannot be described by any image and He is not restricted to any place. He is absolutely in control of all things, never to be brought under the control of man as a physical object. This is why the Bible prohibits any form of description of God in form of idol or graven images (Exodus 20:4).

4. God is Holy. One of the most fundamental features of God's being is expressed by the word *holy*. He is the incomparable God, 'the Holy One" (Isaiah 40:25; cf. Habakkuk 3:3). "Holy", which in both Hebrew and Greek has the root meaning of separateness, is used predominantly in Scripture for a separation from sin. But this is only a secondary meaning derived from the primary application of God's separateness from all creation, i.e., his transcendence. "He is exalted over all the nations." Therefore, "he is holy" (Psalm99:2-3). He is "the high and lofty One . . . whose name is holy," and he lives "in a high and holy place" (Isaiah 57:15). In his holiness God is the transcendent Deity.[138]

God's transcendence expresses the truth that God in himself is infinitely exalted above all creation. The concept of revelation presupposes a transcendent God who must unveil himself to be known . . . On the other hand, it is biblically incorrect to conceive of God in his transcendence as existing in a realm of timeless nowhereness outside of creation. In a manner that exceeds our finite understanding, God exists in his own infinite realm as transcendent Lord over all creaturely time and space.[139]

However, contrary to what deists believe, God did not set the universe in motion and left it to run itself; God's presence pervades His creation. Though distinct from the universe, God's transcendent holiness is biblically balanced with His immanence.

---

[138] Horton 91-2

[139] Ibid

By immanence we mean God's nearness to His entire creation. Isaiah explains: "For this is what the high and lofty One says— he who lives forever, whose name is holy: "I live in a high and holy place, *but also with him who is contrite and lowly in spirit . . .*" (Isa. 57:15; emphasis mine).

The biblical concept of God's immanence counters the deism and must not be confused with pantheism. God is transcendent and immanent. He guides, governs, protects, sustains and provides for His creation (Hebrews 1:3). He is immanent in all human history. Psalm 139:1-10 provides a more powerful witness to His immanence. The Psalmist expresses God's nearness in this manner: ". . . He is familiar with all my ways (vs. 3); where can I go from your Spirit? Where can I flee from your presence? If I go up to the heavens, you are there; If I make my bed in the depths, you are there . . . your hand will guide me, your right hand will hold me fast" (vs. 7, 8, 10). Ultimately, the incarnation of Jesus bears strong witness to the immanence of God—He is Immanuel, "God with us". In summary, God is omnipotent, omnipresent, omniscient, eternal, infinite, holy, merciful, and He is love.

The Uniqueness of Christianity

Having considered the concepts of God in African religions, Islam and Christianity, one may be tempted to say the three dominant religions in Africa believe in the same God, since the three seems to share similar views of God. This is not true. Some Christians say, "Christianity and Islam are the same, believing in one God. Only the way and manner of worship differentials us." This is a mistake no Christian should make. Though Muslims reject idols and believe in only one God as Christians do, this does not mean their beliefs are the same. We must understand that Muslim worldviews differ largely from ours.

However, the uniqueness of Christianity is found in its claims about God, Christ, the Bible, the doctrine of Trinity, and the way of salvation. Surrounded by an ocean of religions in the world, Christianity towers above them all.

- **A Unique View of God.** Islamic religion teaches the oneness but rejects Christian teaching on the fatherhood of God. According to Jesus, God is our Father, yet the Qur'an specifically denies that Allah is a father (sura 112:1-4; 5:18). The fatherhood of God is perceived by Muslims to mean a physical fatherhood. This makes Muslims feel it is bringing God too low if we compare Him with human being such as a father. Interestingly, Jesus taught us to call Him Father (in the spiritual sense), to show the greatness of God's love for us. Just as a human father will care for his children, God as a Father cares for each one of us, protects us, defends us, forgives us when we err, and provides for us. He cares for us far more that the best human father cares for his children.

Another subject that points to the unique view of God is the Christian teaching of God as a triune being. This is certainly one of the most important battlegrounds in the history of the church. No other religion in human history is explicitly Trinitarian. The New Testament incorporates Jesus Christ and the

Holy Spirit into the oneness of God, but the Qur'an excludes both.

This doctrine of Trinity has been mistakenly thought to mean Tri-theism—a belief in three gods. Tri-theism is absolutely against what the Bible teaches about God. R. A. Finlayson explains the concept of Trinity in this manner: "God is one in His essential being, but the 'divine essence' exists in three modes or forms, each constituting a Person, yet in such a way that the divine essence is wholly in each person."[140]

The development of this doctrine owes much to three of the early Fathers of the church—Iranaeus, Tertullian and Origen. According to Finlayson, "Under the leadership of Athanasius the doctrine was proclaimed as the faith of the church at the Council of Nicaea (A.D. 325), and at the hand of Augustine a century later it received a formulation, enshrined the so-called Athanasian Creed."[141]

---

[140] R.A Finlayson, "Trinity" *New Bible Dictionary* (Downers Grove, Illinois: InterVarsity Press, 1962), 1298

[141] Ibid

The trinity is a difficult concept and one of the causes of the problem of understanding the trinity as identified by Paul E. Little is "the inadequacy of human words to express divine reality." For instance, we speak of the "Persons" in the Godhead. We use this term because it describes a being who has intellect, emotion, and will. We can understand this. But we must be careful in applying such terms to God.[142] "Three persons" is the usual expression, but it is an imperfect term, denoting separate moral or rational individuals. There are not three individuals but *three personal self-distinctions* within *one* divine essence.[143]

"Person" used in human terms implies independence, not oneness of will, actions, and feelings as is true of the Trinity. The Divine Trinity is one self-conscious, self-directing being, yet no part ever acts independently, or in opposite to the others. God is a

---

[142] Paul E. Little, *Know What You Believe* (IVP Books, Downers Grove, Illinois, 2008), 30

[143] Ibid

unity; His life is not split into three. He is one in essence, in personality, and will.[144]

Creation account of Genesis shows us the activities of the Trinity in creation: God the Father created the world, through the Son, by the Holy Spirit. The Son and the Spirit are subordinate to the Father but they are in no way inferior to Him. There subordination is a matter of relationship, not of nature.

Salvation also clearly portrays the work of the triune God. Salvation was God's initiative, which He sent the Son to accomplish by His death. The Son sent the Spirit to bring conviction and apply to people's heart what Christ has accomplished through His death and resurrection. The Trinity is essential to the Christian faith and especially to the doctrine of salvation. Without the Trinity, incarnation (the doctrine that God assumed human form in the person of Jesus, the second person of the Trinity, and is fully divine and fully human) wouldn't have been possible. Without Jesus Christ, who is God incarnate, there

---

[144] Ibid

would be no salvation from sin. Without salvation, sin would condemn all to eternal hell.

Nevertheless, the subordination of the Son and the Spirit to the Father does not indicate any form of inferiority. The three persons of the Godhead are of equal divine essence. Although in the economy of the trinity, each one has a specific role to play, yet, no one acts independently, or in opposition to the others—there is *oneness* of will, purpose, actions and feelings.

Also worthy of note is the truth that the Bible assigns deity to the Son and the Spirit, just as the Father. Of the Son the Bible clears says He is God's incarnate (John 1:14), the image of the invisible God (Col. 1:13), God our Saviour (Titus 3:4), and the exact representation of God's being, sustaining all things by His powerful word (Hebrews 1:3). Of the Spirit, Peter regarded Him as God, believing that lying to Him is lying to God (Acts 5:3-4). Therefore, the Son (Jesus Christ) and the Holy Spirit must not be reduced below the level of strict deity. They are not lesser form of deity. The Son and the Holy Spirit are coequal and co-eternal with the Father.

Only in the Christian Trinity is there one God in essence who is expressed eternally in three distinct persons—Father, Son, and Holy Spirit (Matthew 28:18-19). The Islamic view of God is false because it insists that there is only one person in the godhead.[145] For more reference, read the following Bible verses about the Trinity: Matthew 28:19; Luke 3:21-22; John 15:26; 2 Corinthians 13:14.

- **The Uniqueness of the Bible.** The Bible is one of the most quoted and misunderstood books in the world, yet its relevance cannot be denied. It is a unique book because its impact on lives has been tremendous and fascinating. Its live-changing ability has given it edge over other books in the world.

The Bible is God's word, inspired by the Holy Spirit, but spoken and written in human language. It is the revelation of God to man, documented by the holy men of old, for the purpose of communicating His will and intents to mankind and to also instruct man about to live. It contains 66 books, written by about 40 authors, in three different languages (Hebrew and

---
[145] Horton, 421

Aramaic languages for the O.T, and Greek for the N.T), within the space of fifteen hundred (1,500) years.

The authors of the Bible wrote at different times and represented different professions and walks of life. Among the writers we have a farmer (Amos), shepherds (Moses and David), government leaders (Moses and Joshua), civil servants (Daniel and Nehemiah), kings (David and Solomon), musicians (Asaph, Ethan, David, etc.), prophets (Isaiah, Jeremiah, and many others), a professional Scribe (Ezra), fishermen (Peter and John), tax collector (Matthew), rabbi (Paul), physician (Luke) and a carpenter (Probably James the brother of Jesus).

Interestingly, these writers represent a wide range of background, but the Bible is a unified whole, as Jesus being the central theme of the Bible. Tyrants had burned the Bible and secular scholars have subjected the Bible to a relentless intellectual scrutiny and debates. Yet, the Bible remains indestructible; it remains the bestseller of all times.

The Bible is unique in its teachings. No ancient or modern book tells us so much about the origin, nature, and the destiny of man like the Bible. It doesn't conceal the sins and failure of its heroes, but reveals them and frankly deals with them—Noah's drunkenness, Abraham's cowardice and lies, Jacob's deception, Moses' disobedience, David's adultery and murder and Peter's denying his Master and his hypocrisy—all were recorded in the Bible.

Through the Bible we have learned so much about the attribute and nature of God, how we are related to Him, what He expects of us, and what the purpose of life is. The Bible has helped us to answer many of our important questions like, "where did I come from"? "Who am I"? "What is my future like"? The Bible provides answers to these questions.

Furthermore, the uniqueness of the Bible is also seen in its historical and prophetic contents. Skeptics have tried to discredit, seeking where the Bible erred in its historical contents, but archeologist and even secular historians have made more for claims for the historical accuracy and authenticity of the Bible. The Bible also contains a large body of prophecies concerning cities, individuals, Israel, the Messiah, the

Church and the world at large, of which many have been fulfilled already.

Below are some Old Testament Messianic Prophecies and their Fulfillments:

O.T Messianic Prophecies	Fulfillments in the N.T
1. Gen. 3:15 (Seed of a woman)	Galatians 4:4-5; Mt. 1:18; Heb.2:14; 1 John 3:8
2. Ps. 2:7,8 (crucifixion and resurrection)	Acts 3:29-33
3. Ps. 16:10 (not to see corruption)	Acts 2:31; 13:35
4. Ps. 16:9-11 (was to rise from the dead)	John 20:9
5. Ps. 22:16 (they pierced His hand and feet)	John 19:34, 37; 20:27
6. Ps. 22:31 (they parted His garment)	John 19:23, 24
7. Isa. 7:14 (born of a virgin)	Lk. 1:35; Mt. 1:18-23
8. Micah 5:2a (born in Bethlehem)	Mt. 2:1-6
9. Zech. 9:9 (presented to Jerusalem riding on a donkey)	Mt. 21:6-9
10. Zech. 11:12-13a (betrayed for thirty pieces of silver)	Mt. 26:14-15

In Matthew 24:7, Jesus predicted the future and the signs of the end of age: "For nation will rise against nation, and kingdom against kingdom. And there will be famines, pestilences, and earthquakes in various places". Consider the increase of earthquakes in history:

In the fifteenth century there were 115 earthquakes.

In the sixteenth century there were 253 earthquakes.

In the seventeenth century there were 378 earthquakes.

In in eighteenth century there were 640 earthquakes.

In the nineteenth century there were 2,119 earthquakes.

In the twentieth century earthquakes happened with such rapidity and regularity that tremors are considered "life as usual" in California.[146]

No founders of religions, whether Confucius, Buddha, Muhammad, Zoroaster or Ifa oracle foretold the future with such accuracy as the Bible. They do know the future, neither can they bring to pass what

---

[146] John Hagee, *The Seven Secrets* (Florida: Charisma House, 2004), 171

has been spoken aforetime, but the fulfilled prophecies of the Bible bespeak the omniscience of its divine author— God. The Bible is the only reliable book of prophecy.

- **The Uniqueness of Jesus Christ.** The ultimate uniqueness of Christianity stems from the uniqueness of Jesus Christ.

The African continent had benefitted immensely from Christianity. Being a continent with a long standing history of poverty, insecurity, religious and political violence, terrorism, social injustices, infant mortality, and other social vices, Christianity has offered hope and shared the love of Jesus to millions of Africans through various gospel outreaches and aids.

Christian missionaries have provided shelters to displayed persons, built free schools and medical centers for those who could not afford them, provided dresses for those who would have been naked, taught young people new skills to help them fend for themselves, dug wells and borehole waters in various villages, and brought life back to communities that have been deserted for fear of terrorism. Christianity has brought spiritual and moral transformation to Africa.

Matthew Parris, an atheist and conservative member of the parliament from 1979 to 1986 has this to say about Christian exploits in Africa:

> . . . A confirmed atheist, I've become convinced of the enormous contribution that Christian evangelism makes in Africa: sharply distinct from the work of secular NGOs, government projects and international aid efforts. These alone will not do. In Africa Christianity changes people's hearts. It brings a spiritual transformation. The rebirth is real. The change is good. . .whenever we entered a territory worked by missionaries, we had to acknowledge that something changed in the faces of the people we passed and spoke to: something in their eyes, the way they approached you direct, man-to-man, without looking down or away. They had not become more deferential towards strangers—in some ways less so—but more open." He concluded: "Removing Christian evangelism from African equation may leave the continent at the mercy of a malign fusion of Nike, the witch doctor, the mobile phone and the machete.[147]

In his excellent book, *What If Jesus had Never Been Born?*, James Kennedy gives an overview of

---

[147] Dennis Prince, *I Was Wrong* (Florida: Creation House, 2013), 6-7.

some of the positive contributions Christianity has made throughout the centuries. Here are few highlights:

- Hospitals, which essentially began during the Middle Ages.
- Universities, which also began during the Middle Ages. In addition, most of the world's greatest universities were started by Christians for Christian purposes.
- Literacy and education for the masses.
- Capitalism and free enterprise.
- Representative government, particularly as it has been seen in the American experiment.
- The separation of political powers.
- Civil liberties.
- The abolition of slavery, both in antiquity and in more modern times.
- Modern science.
- The elevation of women.
- Benevolence and charity; the good Samaritan ethic.
- Higher standard of justice.
- The elevation of common man.

- The civilizing of many barbarian and primitive cultures.
- The condemnation of adultery, homosexuality, and other sexual perversions. This has helped to preserve the human race, and it has spared many from heartache.
- High regard for human life.
- The codifying and setting to writing of many of the world's languages.
- Greater development of art and music. The inspiration for the greatest works of art.
- The countless changed lives transformed from liabilities into assets to society because of the gospel.
- The eternal salvation of countless souls![148]

The above are possible only because of Jesus Christ, because there is no Christianity without Jesus Christ.

Buddha is not essential to the teaching of Buddhism, or Muhammad to Islam, but everything about Christianity is determined by the person and work of Jesus Christ. Christianity owes its life,

---

[148] *The Uniqueness of Jesus Christ*, https://bible.org/article/uniqueness-jesus-christ (accessed October 7, 2019)

substance, and character in every detail to Christ. He was: the author of its teachings, the object of its doctrine, the origin of its salvation, the fulfillment of its hopes, the source of its power, the founder of its church, and the one who gave the Holy Spirit as a legacy to those who believe.[149]

Jesus is unique in all ramifications: His birth was unique, He lived a unique life, His teachings are unique, His death was unique, His resurrection was unique and His return shall be unique also.

i. *The Uniqueness of His Birth.* Great leaders were born before Jesus, but His birth was unique and incomparable. Centuries before His birth, prophets predicted His birth and men waited in earnest anticipation for the unique Son of God to come into the world. He was conceived and born of a virgin, a miracle which history has not been able to replicate.

His birth was so unique that it had to be announced by an angel. Great company of the heavenly host and the shepherds who were keeping watch over their flocks at night worshipped God for

---
[149] Little, 37

the birth of Son of God. Who among neither the great men of old nor the prophets received such an angelic annunciation and adoration? History bears no record of any king, Emperor, warrior or warlord who accrued so much expectation from men like Jesus the Christ. Moses laid the foundation for His coming in the Law; the prophets wrote with earnest expectations, longing to see the one who they prophesied about and biblical poets were loaded with aspirations for the Son of God.

Though born a tributary, Herod recognized Him as a more superior King than himself. Without telegraph, Facebook, mobile phone, Twitter or any other social and traditional media, the birth of Jesus was known by the Magi from the east, and they traveled all the way to worship the one who was born King of the Jews.

His birth split time in two: two thousand years ago the birth of Jesus Christ rocked the world. His birth changed its calendar and tailored its mores. The atheist dates his checks, thereby declaring Christ's birth. The rulers of countries both east and west, regardless of their religions, use His birth date.

Unthinkingly, we declare His birth on letters, legal documents, and datebooks.[150]

ii. *The Uniqueness of His Life.* Another unique feature found in Jesus Christ was His very life. Though He was hated and vehemently criticized by the religious leaders of His time, His moral attributes remained impeccable. He gave both the nobles and the social outcast equal attention. He was utterly approachable and patient with the weak. He offered Himself a Shepherd to wanderers, leading them and showing them the way to eternal rest. He would not send the poor away without meeting his most urgent need. His fed the hungry with the food they needed for spiritual and physical survival, gave hope to the hopeless, wiped tears away, defended the poor and stood against social ills. He related indiscriminately with people of all classes and social status. He was a friend to tax collectors, fishermen, peasants, and also gave audience to the upper class.

One of His favorite disciples testified of how He went around doing good and healing all who were

---

[150] Little, *Know What You Believe*, 41

under the power of the devil (Acts 10:38). He showed no preference for the rich over the poor; for to Him, all men are equal before God. Interestingly, no single sin was credited to His moral account. Hebrews 4:15 says "He was tempted in every way, just as we are — yet without sin." Also worthy of note is the testimony of the apostle Peter that "He committed no sin, and no deceit was found in his mouth" (1 Peter 2:22). He never prayed for [His own] forgiveness and He confidently challenged the dissenters to convict Him of any known sin. No religious leader anywhere has such a clean bill like Jesus Christ. He lived His entire life for the wellbeing of others, and ultimately gave His life as ransom for many (Mark 10:45).

iii. *The Uniqueness of His Teachings*. Jesus is incontrovertibly the greatest teacher of all times. He taught with so much authority, simplicity and thoroughness. He knew the appropriate lesson to teach per time, the right answers to give inquirers, the best illustrations to drive home His points, and the appropriate teaching method to adopt at every given situation.

His teaching skill held thousands of listeners spellbound, convicted and transformed His listeners. No religious leader taught so much about God, man, sin, eternal judgment, eternal reward, salvation, love, mercy, prayer, forgiveness, and righteousness like Jesus did.

Jesus taught about love like no other man in human history. He taught and demonstrated the power of love. Those before Him taught that a man should love his neighbor and hate his enemy, but He taught that we should love our enemies and pray for those who persecute us (Matthew 5:43-44). In His teachings, Jesus discouraged and taught against divorce, retaliation, adultery and fornication, unforgiveness, violence, bigotry, partiality, hate, injustice, arrogance, gender discrimination, disobedience to God and all constituted authorities. He taught us to give, love, forgive, respect and sacrifice for others. The central theme of His teachings is the kingdom of God and God's willingness to get humanity into His kingdom.

He taught on the reality and certainty of eternity, a place of rest and unimpaired fellowship with God, while Prophet Muhammad, in Qur'an 46:9 expressed uncertainty about his eternal destination: ". . . I do not know what will be done to me or to you." Taking inference of Jesus' teachings, the apostle Paul stated in Ephesians 2:8-9 that Christians are saved by the effort of Christ, not their own, but in Islam, salvation is by good deeds outweighing the bad. Jesus' teachings are unique.

iv. *The Uniqueness of His Death and Resurrection.* Put succinctly, the uniqueness of Christ's death was first revealed in His *willingness* to offer His own life as atonement for sin. The Bible clearly affirms that Jesus *willingly gave* His life for us. He chose to die, so that whosoever receives Him by faith may have eternal life through Him (Phil. 2:6, 8; 1 John 3:16; Matt.20:28). In John 10:17-18, Jesus said: "The reason my Father loves me is that I lay down my life—only to take it again. No-one takes it from me, but I lay it down of my own accord. . . ." While some religious leaders and founders violently shed the blood of those they perceived as dissenters and enemies to gain domination, Jesus shed His own blood and even died for His enemies so that they can come to God (Romans 5:8).

Skeptics have made several attempts to minimize or discount Christ's death on the cross. Most Muslims doubt whether Jesus died on the cross. Some skeptic groups accepted Christ's crucifixion but denied His death on the cross. According to them, Jesus did not actually die; he merely swooned on the cross and laid in the tomb half-dead. They maintained that after three days, the coolness of the tomb revived Him and He managed to roll away the stone, came out of the tomb and appeared to His disciples, making them think He had resurrected. This theory is ludicrous and no sane person will want to dwell on this.

From a historical, logical and medical point of view, it is impossible for Jesus to have survived the crucifixion. British author Michael Green has this to say:

> We are told on eyewitness authority that "blood and water" came out of the pieced side of Jesus (John 19:34-35). The eyewitness clearly attached

great importance to this. Had Jesus been alive when the spear pierced His side, strong spouts of blood would have emerged with every heartbeat. Instead, the observer noticed semi-solid dark red clot seeping out, distinct and separate from the accompanying watery serum. This is evidence of massive clotting of the blood in the main arteries, and is exceptionally strong medical proof of death. It is all the more impressive because the evangelist could not possibly have realized its significance to a pathologist. The "blood and water" from the spear-thrust is proof positive that Jesus was already dead.[151]

Dr. C. Truman Davis in *A Physician's View of the Crucifixion of Jesus Christ* also has this to say:
Jesus experienced hours of limitless pain, cycles of twisting, joint-rending cramps, intermittent partial asphyxiation, searing pain where tissue is torn from the lacerated back as He moves up and down against the rough timber. Then another agony begins— a terrible crushing pain deep in the chest as the pericardium slowly fills with serum and begins to compress the heart.[152]

There are also other biblical proofs that Jesus did not swoon but actually died. The Roman executioners

---

[151] Michael Green, *Man Alive* (Downers Grove, IL: InterVarsity Press, 1968), 33

[152] Truman Davis, *A Physician's View of the Crucifixion of Jesus Christ*. www1.cbn.com (accessed October 13, 2019)

believed that Jesus died right on the cross (John 19:33); the Roman centurion also attested to His death (Mark 5:44-55); blood and water flowed from His side, signaling a ruptured heart (John 19:34); Joseph Arimathaea sought Pilate's permission to bury Jesus, showing that he believed Jesus was already dead (Mark 15:43); the women who had stood by His cross believed He died (Mark 16:1); His disciples believed He died (Acts 3:14-15); Paul who was formally hostile to the gospel believed Jesus died (1 Corinthians 15:3); ultimately, Jesus Himself said He died (Revelation 1:18). Even liberal scholars like John Dominic Crossan believe the execution of Jesus is as certain as any historical fact can be.[153]

The death was not an accident of history. He did not die just to show us example; His death provided atonement for sin. Jesus died on behalf of sinners so that through faith in Him, sinners can be forgiven, saved, redeemed, restored and reconciled to God. His death healed man's estrangement from God and made

---

[153] John Dominic Crossan, *Who Killed Jesus?* (New York: Harper Collins, 1996), 33

fellowship with God possible. The wrath and displeasure of God was removed as Christ shed His precious blood on the Cross, rendering God propitious to His people.

The death of Jesus was necessary because man's disobedience to God separated man from His Maker. The consequences which God had warned Adam and Eve of involved physical and spiritual death, that is, separation from their Maker. Paul Little summarized the results thus:

- The image of God in man was badly marred in both its moral and its natural dimensions;
- Man lost his original inclination toward God;
- Man's desires inclined away from his Creator; and
- Man's intellect became bound, his emotions corrupted, and his will enslaved.[154]

Furthermore, God's holiness would not allow Him to simply overlook sin; His justice must be maintained (Exodus 34:6-7; Romans 3: 25-26). And because of the immutability of His law, which is a reflection of His

---

[154] Little, *Know What You Believe*, 71

very nature, it is necessary for Him to demand satisfaction of the sinners, having declared that death would be the penalty on either the offender or the substitute, and He must stay true to His word (Numbers 23:19; Romans 3:4). Therefore, Christ offered Himself as *the* substitute; He procured and secured man's redemption through His death—since man is incapable in every respect to save himself and he could not meet the righteous requirements of God—Jesus died in his stead.

The *just* God must judge every sin; so He judged man sins on Jesus, who *voluntarily* offered Himself as penalty for sin. Therefore, through the death of Jesus, the estrangement from our Creator has been healed; we are ransomed, redeemed, redeemed, forgiven, and we can be adopted into the family of God.

On the final note, of what good is the death of Jesus without His resurrection from the death? The truth of His resurrection offers mankind the greatest hope. His death demonstrated His love, but His resurrection demonstrated His power—". . . it was *impossible* for death to keep its hold on Him" (Acts 2:24b, emphasis mine).

The resurrection of Jesus is the single most important event in human history. It is the focus of the Christian faith; it is where our hope rests. Without His resurrection, the apostle Paul said:

(a). our preaching is useless (1 Cor. 15:14);

(b). our faith is vain (vs.14);

(c). the apostles are false witnesses about God (vs.15);

(d). believers are yet in their sins (vs. 17);

(e). the dead in Christ are perished (vs. 18).

The implications of the resurrection of Jesus are enormous. His resurrection is what fully confirms the truth and validity of what Jesus taught. It is the greatest proof of His divinity. Also of a great benefit to believers in Christ is the fact that Christ's resurrection is the *guarantee* of their own resurrection too. Believers shall one day wear a glorified body like Jesus— a body free from pains, diseases, weakness, decay, deterioration and the agony of death.

In conclusion, in spite of the apparent religious plurality in Africa, I agree with the sentiment of F.F

Bruce that *Christianity is the religion*—the final and true religion.

CHAPTER TEN

Who Do Men Say I Am?

"Who do men say I am," Jesus asked His disciples. Thousands of scholars and religious leaders had made several attempts to provide answers to this straightforward but complex question. To some, He is just a mythical hero, and to another, He is but one of the prophets. The religious leaders of His time called Him a mad man (John 10:20, NIV). Although, one of His disciples provided an instant answer to the question by saying, He is the Son of the living God, but skeptics deny the authenticity of the biblical records of the life and ministry of Jesus.

A good number of myths and literature have been published over the years to disprove the historical testimony and the personality of Jesus. Many notable scholars and influential leaders often look for the ground to make people not to believe anything about

Jesus, let alone his divinity. The biblical claims of his virgin birth, His miracles, His death and His resurrection have been considered a myth by the skeptics and even some so-called "Christians" deny the divinity of Jesus.

Ayman al-Zawahiri, the leader of Al-Qaeda even took time out from excoriating George W. Bush and Pope Benedict XVI in a 2006 video tape to urge all Christians to convert to Islam, which, he said, correctly believes that Jesus was never put to death, never rose from the dead, and was never divine.[155] Al-Zawahiri's conclusion about the death, resurrection, and divinity of Jesus shows his level of intellectual naivety. His presupposition was not based on facts and his conclusion has no form of honesty in it. It is rather the revelation of ignorance on his part and his conclusion shows a willful unbelief.

Jesus Christ is so firmly embedded into world history that no knowledgeable and educated person can conceivably question his historicity. The four

---

[155] Lee Strobel, *The Case For The Real Jesus* (Grand Rapids, Michigan: Zondervan, 2007), 102

gospels (Matthew, Mark, Luke and John) provides detailed historical narratives about the Lord Jesus, but due to various attacks by skeptics and disputers who would not want to accept the biblical claims of His historicity, there are many other extra-biblical materials available to prove the historicity of Jesus. N.T Wright, in *The Challenge of Jesus* writes:

> If Christianity is not rooted in things that actually happened in first century Palestine, we might as well be Buddhists, Marxists, or almost anything else. And if Jesus never existed, or if he was quite different from what the Gospels and the church's worship affirm him to have been, then we are indeed living in cloud-cuckoo-land. The skeptics can and must be answered.[156]

The synoptic gospels gives a detailed account of His birth, His genealogy, the circumstances that surrounded His birth, the place of His birth, the season, the government during His birth, and affirms that His birth was a fulfillment of a prophecy spoken long ago in the Old Testament.

---

[156] N.T Wright, *The Challenge of Jesus: Rediscovering Who Jesus Was and Is* (Downers Grove, IL: InterVarsity Press, 1999), 18

A good number of passages in the Old Testament informs us of the prophecy regarding His birth and the mission He came to fulfill prophet Isaiah prophesied his virgin birth and His divine origin (Isaiah 7:14, 9:6). Christian scholar Paul Feinberg declares, "I have a special love for Jesus because he is the fulfillment of the prophecies to my people, the Jews." However, critics claim several flaws regarding the prophecy concerning Jesus' virgin birth spoken of by prophet Isaiah. First, they say the word Isaiah used to describe the mother, '*almah*', does not mean "virgin"—and if he had wanted to convey the idea of virginity, he would have used a better word '*betulah*'.[157]

Michael L. Brown, in his conversation with Lee Strobel gave a satisfying clarity on this matter: "To be precise", Brown said "almah" really deals with "Youthfulness". Brown continues, "Four other times when the word is used elsewhere in the Old Testament, the New International Version doesn't translate it as 'virgin'. However, the foremost Jewish

---

[157] Ibid., 217

commentator Rashi said, 'And some interpret that this is the sign that she was a young girl'—an '*almah*'—and incapable of giving birth".[158]

Some Jewish experts interpreted the text to mean that God's sign to Ahaz had to be with the highly unusual nature of the birth. Here was a young girl, an *'almah'*, for whom giving birth would not be normal. The birth itself was unusual perhaps even supernatural.[159] Scholars and many skeptics over the past decades had made vigorous efforts to disregard the biblical accounts regarding the historicity Jesus and the identity of Jesus. Lee Strobel, in his book titled *The Case for the Real Jesus*, enumerated various challenges Christians face on the identity of Jesus. The Challenges goes thus:

1. Scholars are uncovering a radically different Jesus in ancient documents just as credible as the four gospels.

---

[158] Ibid., 218

[159] Ibid

2. The Bible's portrait of Jesus cannot be trusted because the Church tampered with the text.

3. New explanations have refuted Jesus resurrection

4. Christianity's beliefs about Jesus were copied from pagan religions.

5. Jesus was an imposter who failed to fulfill the messianic prophecies.

6. People should be free to choose what to believe about Jesus.[160]

Also, *The Jesus Seminar* in 1996 asserts that "Jesus . . . is an imaginative theological construct".[161] All of these were meant to discredit the biblical account of the historical Jesus. Fortunately, there are many extra-biblical evidences for the existence of Christ.

The Christ Myth Theory

Myths are not stories based on facts and they are equally not expected to be hundred percent true. This

---

[160] Ibid

[161] Timothy Paul Jones, *Conspiracies And The Cross* (Florida: FrontLine, 2008), 2

is exactly what skeptics and other radical scholars feel about the historicity of Jesus. They consider every biblical record that affirms the existence of Christ as the fabricated stories of his loyal followers and adherents. To these scholars, the synoptic gospels' accounts of the birth, genealogy, miracles, teachings, crucifixion, resurrection, and the ascension of Christ is nothing but a myth.

Christ myth theory denies the existence of Jesus Christ as a physical historical figure, and only regard Christ as a mere mythical hero. This theory maintains that Christ was a mythical hero or incorporeal character created by the early Christian community, but presented to the world as a real historical figure. The early proponents of this theory are: Charles Francois Dupuis, Constantin Francois Volney, David Strauss, Edwin Johnson, Dutch Radical School, Thomas Whittaker, etc. These men blatantly questioned the existence of Jesus of Nazareth.[162]

---

[162] https://en.wikipedia.org/wiki/christ-myth-theory (accessed July 19, 2018)

If these men deny the existence of Jesus of Nazareth as a historical figure, they automatically deny the entirety of his life story as described in the four gospels. In other words, the story of his life is of no use if He never existed at all. Another variant holds that there was a person called Jesus, but almost all the teachings and miracles attributed to him were either invented or symbolic references. Yet another version suggests that the Jesus portrayed in the New Testament is a composite character constructed from multiple people over a period of time.[163]

The group that holds that there was a person called Jesus but rejects all his teachings and miracles attributed to him is in another way saying, "We agree that there was a man called Jesus, but all the teachings and miracles attributed to him are just too much for a mortal to accept." They sarcastically accept His existence but deny his teachings, miracles, and all his personal claims.

---

[163] Ibid

Most myth theories use arguments based on variants of three main components: first, that the New Testament accounts have no historical value; secondly, an argument from silence based on the absence of references to Jesus in contemporary non-Christian sources, and combined various myths to build the gospel accounts.[164]

The proponents of these theories built their premises on sentiments, and not on sincere historical facts. Christianity is a historical religion and it is therefore open for investigation and verification. The historical aspect of Christianity is very important and undeniably relevant to its faith. Barth Ehrman has stated that now virtually all scholars of antiquity agree that Jesus existed, and Robert M. Price agrees that this denial perspective runs against the views of the majority of scholars. Also, myth theorist G.A. Wells has also softened hesitance on the non-existence issue.[165]

---

[164] Ibid

[165] Ibid

The Trustworthiness of the New Testament

Is the New Testament worthy of acceptance by Christians and non-Christians as a reliable source of information about Christ and Christianity? Is the New Testament historically accurate and reliable? How much can we believe its claims about Jesus? These are the questions that sometimes cross our minds as believers in Christ, and non-believers also seem to have some doubts about the historical accuracy of the New Testament, especially in matters that relates to the person of Jesus. Here's how a critic describes the New Testament:

> [The New Testament Gospels] were written thirty-five to sixty-five years after Jesus' death . . . not by people who were eyewitnesses, but by people living later. . . . Where did these people get their information from? . . . After the days of Jesus, people started telling stories about him in order to convert others to the faith. . . . The Gospels of the New Testament contain . . . stories that may convey truths, at least in the minds of those who told them, but that are not historically accurate. Stories based on eyewitness accounts are not necessarily reliable, and the same is true a hundredfold for accounts that—even if stemming from reports of

eyewitnesses—have been in oral circulation long after the fact.[166]

Contrary to the above assertions, the Bible itself and several archaeological discoveries in the recent times had really helped us to further confirm the historical accuracy of the New Testament. Interestingly, the New Testament record of Jesus claims to have been written by eyewitnesses or those closely associated with them.

- 2 Peter 1:16 says, "We did not follow cleverly invented stories when we told you about the power and coming of our Lord Jesus Christ, but we were eyewitnesses of his majesty" (NIV).
- Acts 2:32 says, "God has raised this Jesus to life, and we are all witnesses of the fact" (NIV).
- 1 John 1:1 says, "That which was from the beginning, which we have heard, which we have seen with our eyes, which we have looked at and our hands have touched—this we proclaim concerning the Word of life" (NIV).

---

[166]Jones, 92

From the book co-authored by Norman L. Geisler & William E. Nix titled, *From God to Us*, the following thought may be helpful:

> The history of the New Testament canon differs from that of the Old in several respects. In the first place, since Christianity was an international religion from the beginning, there was no tightly knit prophetic community which received all inspired books and collected them in one place. Local and somewhat complete collections were made from the very beginning, but there is no evidence of a central and official cleaning house for inspired writings. Hence, the process by which all the apostolic writings became universally accepted took many centuries. Fortunately, because of the availability of source materials there is more data available on the New Testament canon than the Old. The New Testament claims to have been written by eye-witnesses or people who have direct contact with the eye-witnesses of the life and ministry of Christ. The authors of the New Testament wrote with great sense of conviction and their records often claim the right to be accepted as the truth.[167]

Around A.D. 200, Tertullian of Carthage also declared:

---

[167] Norman L. Geisler and William E. Nix, *From God to Us* (Chicago: Moody Press, 1974), 101

> We present as our first position, that the Gospel testimony has apostles for its authors, to whom the Lord himself assigned the position of propagating the Gospel. There are also some that, though not *apostles*, are *apostolic*—they do not stand alone; they appear with and after the apostles. . . . So, John and Matthew, of the apostles, first instill faith into us while the apostolic writers Luke and Mark renew it afterwards. . . .Never mind that there occurs some variation in the order of their narratives, as long as there is agreement in essential matters of faith.[168]

Even the critical German scholar Peter Stuhlmacher once said: "We have good reasons to treat the Gospels seriously as a source of information on the life and teachings of Jesus, and thus on the historical origins of Christianity."[169]

Hank Hanegraaff of the Christian Research Institute makes a strong case for the Bible's reliability, using three areas of evidence:

1. **Manuscript Evidence**. The New Testament documents have stronger manuscript support than any

---

[168] Jones, 99

[169] Lee Strobel and Garry Poole, *Exploring The Da Vinci Code* (Grand Rapids, Michigan: Zondervan, 2006), 53

other work of classical literature, including works of Homer, Plato, Aristotle, Caesar, and Tacitus. Furthermore, the reliability of the Gospel accounts is confirmed through eyewitness credentials of the authors. Finally, secular historians—including Josephus (before AD 100), the Roman Tacitus (c. A.D 120), the Roman Suetonius (c. AD 110), and the Roman governor Pliny the Younger (c. AD 110)—confirm many of events, people, places, and customs chronicled in the New Testament.

2. Archaeological Evidence. Archaeology is a powerful witness to the accuracy of the biblical documents, confirming scores of references.

3. Evidence from Messianic Prophecies. The Bible records predictions of events that could not have been known or predicted by chance or common sense.[170]

The Divinity and Humanity of Jesus

The subject of Christ's divinity and humanity have created very alarming debates and controversies over

---

[170] Strobel and Poole, 45

the years, so much that the conclusions of such debates have given birth to denominational biases and hostility. The subject remains one of the greatest challenges of Christian theology and other religious settings had also indicated their interest in knowing the position of Christians in regard to the divinity and the humanity of Jesus.

Many Christian theologians seem not to give affirmative conclusion about the divinity and of Jesus. The orthodox theologians hold an opinion different from the liberal and Neo-Evangelical scholars. The issues of Christ's divinity and humanity therefore seem not to have a final conclusion and coherence among scholars.

Founders of Christian denominations also have different views concerning the divinity and humanity of Jesus, and this had torn Christians apart. The early church fathers also form their own established presupposition regarding the person of Christ. To some, Christ is purely God and has no human trait in Him. To some still, Christ is inferior to God because of

His subordination to the father; while to others, Christ is hundred percent God and hundred perfect human.

Therefore, the purpose of this section is to establish Christ's divinity and humanity in line with the biblical evidences of His claims as God and His life as a man. Was Christ both divine and human? What affirms His deity? What did Jesus say about His deity? And what did the apostles and the early Church Fathers say about His divinity and humanity?

The Divinity of Jesus

The subject of the deity of Christ comes with the questions "Is Christ God?" This remains one of the most controversial discuss among Christian theologians, rationalists, radicals and religious scholars around the world. The deity of Christ has been denied by many religious leaders and even some Christian groups. T.C. Hammond maintains: "This is one of the most important battle grounds in the history of the Church, and no true Christian should for a moment tolerate any description of our master other than that which assigns to Him the fullest deity, co-equal and co-eternal with the Father".[171]

As stated earlier, the Ebionites denied the deity of Jesus in the second century of the Church and asserted that Christ only attained a measure of divinity through His relationship with God. Charles Russell, the founder of the Jehovah's Witnesses also denied the deity of the only begotten of God in a way, and claimed His inferiority to God. Unitarianism, Mormonism and some other movement denied the divinity of Jesus and assigned Jesus a nature and position below that of true deity.[172] Worse than what should be heard of any Christian group, the Jehovah's Witnesses affirmatively concludes that Jesus is the same with Archangel Michael. They insist: "So Michael the archangel is Jesus in his pre-human existence. After his resurrection and return to heaven, Jesus resumed his service as Michael, the Chief angel, "to

---

[171] Paul E. Little, *Know What You Believe* (Nigeria: StillWaters Publications, 2003), 32

[172] Strobel, 102

the glory of God the Father".[173] Without mincing words, it is heretic to equate Jesus, the one whom all the angels worship, with an angel.

The big questions now are: Who is Christ and how is He related to God? What did the human Jesus do and how did the Church come to see Him as God, assigning to Him the titles of divinity? These are the questions I shall give answers to in this section.

To get the ball rolling, Paul's doctrine of *Kenosis* in Philippians 2: 6-11 addresses the hypostatic union of Christ (the teaching that Jesus is fully God and fully man). Colossians 1: 15-23, and 2: 9-10 also presents the Son as the very image (*eikon*) of God and the Creator in whom all the fullness (*pleroma*) of the Godhead dwells bodily. Furthermore, Hebrews 1: 1-3 affirms Christ as the radiance of God's glory and the exact representation of God's nature.

In addition, the epistle to the Hebrews reveals the supremacy of Christ to Angels, to Moses and to Aaron.

---

[173] Matt Slick, *Logical Problem With The Michael Becoming Jesus Who Became Michael Again.* https://carm.org/logical-problem-with-angel-michael-become-jesus-beome-michael (accessed July 25, 2018)

Paul, in his statement about the supremacy of Christ asserts: "For God was pleased to have all his fullness dwell in Him bodily (Col. 1:19). Jesus himself was aware of His divine status when He said He and the Father (God) are one (John 10:30). With the "I AM" sayings, He equated Himself with the God who appeared to Moses in the burning bush (Ex. 3:14).

Jesus realized accomplishments and claimed authority ascribed only to God. He forgave sins (Matt. 9:6) and sent others to do His bidding, claiming all authority "in heaven and on earth" (Matt.28:18-20). The central proclamation of the gospel is that He is the only way to eternal life, a status held by deity alone (John 3:36; 14:6; cp. Acts 4:12; Rom.10:9).

The New Testament pictures Him as worthy of honor and worship due to only deity (John 5:23; Heb.1:6; Rev.5: 12). He is the agent of creation (John1:3) and the mediator of providence (Col.1:17). He raised the dead (John 11:43-44), healed the sick (John 9:6-7), and vanquished demons (Mark 5:13). His resurrection and ascension to heaven also provides evidence for His deity.

The gospel of John makes unique contribution to Christology—the study of the person (Who He is) and the work (what He did/does) of Jesus Christ. Matthew, and Luke narrate events related to the virgin conception and birth of Jesus, while John, in contrast, focuses on the incarnation of the divine Son, the word (*Logos*) of God (John 1: 1-18). The synoptic Christology is "from below", beginning with the birth of Jesus, while John's Christology is "from above", beginning with the preexistent word (*Logos*) who was with God at creation and was God.

The background for John's use of *logos* is the Old Testament concepts of the "word" and "wisdom" (Proverb 8) of God. The word is the agent of creation, the agent of revelation (John 1:4), eternal in nature (John 1:1-2) and the agent of redemption. In Proverbs chapter eight, much of these are the attributes of wisdom—wisdom was with God in the beginning and was present at creation.

John also developed his Christology around seven signs and seven "I AM" sayings, all of which points to the divine nature of the Son. In other words, the miracles and the sayings of Jesus are facts that prove who he is. In John 8:58, Jesus declares Himself to be the "I AM" of the Old Testament. A more direct claim to deity cannot be found aside this.

The Seven "I AM" Statements in John's Gospel

1. I AM the Bread of life – 6:35
2. I AM the light of the word – 8:12
3. I AM the door of the sheep – 10:7
4. I AM the good shepherd – 10:11, 14
5. I AM the resurrection and the life – 11:25
6. I AM the way, the truth, the life – 14:6
7. I AM true vine - 15:1.

The Seven Signs in John's Gospel

1. Jesus turns water into wine – 2: 1-11
2. Jesus heals a nobleman's son – 4:46-54
3. Jesus cures a paralytic – 5: 1- 16
4. Jesus feeds the 5,000 – 6: 1-15
5. Jesus walks on water – 6: 16 -21
6. Jesus heals a blind man – 9: 1-41
7. Jesus raises Lazarus from the dead – 11: 1-57.

The Council of Nicaea asserted that the Son was of one substance with the Father—Jesus was fully divine. Also against the teaching of Eutyches, a monk from Constantinople, who denied that Jesus had two natures, the Council of Chalcedon in AD 451 expressed the Incarnation of Jesus in terms of one person with two natures—human and divine (Hypostatic Union). Contrary to Dan Brown's assertion in *The Da Vinci Code* that Emperor Constantine invented the divinity of Jesus at the Council of Nicaea, the Church Fathers considered Jesus divine long before the Council of Nicaea:

1. Ignatius: "God Himself was manifested in human form" (AD 105).
2. Clement: "It is fitting that you should think of Jesus as of God" (AD 150).
3. Justin Martyr: "Being the first-begotten Word of God, is even God"; Both God and Lord of hosts"; The Father of the universe has a Son.
    And He . . . is even God (AD 160).

4. Irenaeus: "Our Lord, and God, and Savior, and King"; He is God, for the name Emmanuel indicates this" (AD 180).

5. Tertullian: "Christ our God" (AD 200).

6. Origen: "No one should be offended that the Savior is also God" (AD 225).

7. Novatian: "He is not only man, but God also" (AD 235).

8. Cyprian: "Jesus Christ, our Lord and God" (AD 250).

9. Methodius: "He truly was and is . . . with God, and being God" (AD 290).

10. Lactantius: "We believe Him to be God" (AD 304).

11. Arnobius: "Christ performed all these miracles . . . the duty of Divinity" (AD 305).[174]

J.N.D Anderson also stated:

> Similar tributes have been paid by many others who may or may not have professed any personal allegiance to him. Speaking of Alexander, Caesar, Charlemagne and himself, Napoleon wrote: 'I think I understand something of human nature; and I tell you, all these were men, and I am a man: none else is

---

[174] Strobel and Poole, 90

> like Him; Jesus Christ was more than a man. And it is in a similar vein that Raymond Fletcher, an agnostic Member of Parliament and himself an author wrote in *The Guardians* that Christians do not 'need miracles to sustain their beliefs. Christ himself was the miracle'.[175]

The titles ascribed to Jesus provides conclusive evidence for the New Testament's estimate of His person as God: Jesus is 'Lord' (Phil.2:11), "Lord of lords" (I Tim.6:15), "the Lord of glory" (I Cor.2: 8), "the mediator" (Heb. 12:24), and "Who is God over all, blessed forever" (Rom. 9:5). John Stott sums it up:

> So close was his identification with God that it was natural for him to equate a man's attitude to himself with his attitude to God. Thus, to know him was to know God; to see him was to see God; to believe in him was to believe in God; to receive him was to receive God; to hate him was to hate God; to honor him was to honor God.[176]

Therefore, in view of these apparently evidences, I conclude that Jesus is both Lord and God. He is God's *exegesis*.

---

[175] J.N.D Anderson, *Christianity: The Witness Of History* (London: Tyndale Press, 1969), 39

[176] John R. W. Stott, *Basic Christianity* (Downers Grove, Ill.: InterVarsity Press, 1958), 26

The Humanity of Jesus

It should not be concluded yet that Jesus is fully divine without making mention of His humanity. He was also fully human; He was not partially human nor did He function at some times as man and at other times as God. He was fully God and fully human.

These physical and emotional traits along with others mentioned in the gospels demonstrate that the New Testament assumes Jesus real and full humanity. Finally, He bled and died (John 19:33-34). Yet He was not just a real man; He was also a unique man.

Although, the above assertion that Jesus was fully human was denied by Apollinarius, Bishop of Laodicea. Apollinarius insisted that "Jesus was a heavenly man dissimilar to earthly men. If a human is body, soul, and spirit, the bishop asserted that Jesus was a body, soul, and logos (lit "word"), a man not having a human spirit, or mind."[177]

The council of Constantinople met to clarify and refute the Christology of Apollinarius and therefore

---

[177] Trent C. Butler, ed., *Holman Illustrated Bible Dictionary*, 814

affirmed the full humanity of Jesus. A proper understanding of the events preceding and including His death requires an affirmation of His full humanity. In the garden, He prayed for emotional and physical strength to face the critical hours that lay ahead. He perspired as one under great physical strain (Luke 22: 43 -44). In line with the scriptural affirmation of His humanity, the council of Constantinople in AD 381 affirmed His humanity.[178]

The Proofs of His Humanity

The following are the human side of Jesus:

1. He began life as a baby, born from a woman (Luke 2:6-7)

2. He became tired and fatigued (John 4:6; Mark 4:38)

2. He Slept (Matthew 8: 24)

3. He became hunger and thirsty (Matthew 21: 18; John 19:28)

4. Suffering – Luke 22: 43-44

5. Joy (John 15:11)

---

[178] Ibid

Jesus also experienced the emotional reactions of mankind:

1. Compassion (Luke 7:13)
2. Weeping (Luke 19:41)
3. Anger and indignation (Mark 3:5)
4. Grief (Matthew 26: 37).

Extra-biblical Evidence about Jesus

Historical Jesus expert Gary Habermas has argued that "ancient extra-biblical sources do present a surprisingly large amount of detail concerning both the life of Jesus and the nature of early Christianity."[179] He notes that, "Overall, at least seventeen non-Christian writings record more than fifty details concerning the life, teachings, death, and resurrection of Jesus, plus details concerning the earliest church."[180]

1. **FLAVIUS JOSEPHUS** (Born AD 37): Josephus was a Jewish historian who became a Pharisee at age 19;

---

[179] Josh McDowell and Sean McDowell, *Jesus: Dead or Alive?* (California: Regal, 2009), 111

[180] Ibid

in AD 66 he was the commander of Jewish forces in Galilee. After being captured, he was attached to the Roman headquarters. The collected works of Josephus is a massive historical document, more massive than the Bible. It is a valuable reference book for students in ancient history.[181] Josephus in his historical document records:

> Now there was about this Jew, a wise man, if it be lawful to call him a man, for he was a doer of wonderful works, a teacher of such men as receive the truth with pleasure. He drew over to him both many of the Jews, and, many of the Gentiles. He was the Christ, and when Pilate, at the suggestion of the principal men among us, had condemned him to the cross, those that loved him at the first, did not forsake; for he appeared to them alive again the third day; as the divine prophets had foretold these and ten thousand other wonderful thing, concerning him. And the tribes of Christians so named after him are not extinct at this day.[182]

2. **CORNELIUS TACITUS**: (Born around AD 52): He was the dean of Roman historians, and alludes to the

---

[181] Philip and Cherian, 9

[182] Ibid

death of Christ and to the existence of Christians, at Rome:

> But not all the belief that could come from man, not all the bounties that the prince could bestow, nor all the atonements which could be presented to the gods, availed to relieve Nero from the infancy of being believed to have ordered the conflagration, the fire of Rome. Hence to suppress the rumor, he falsely charged with the guilt, and punished with the most exquisite tortured, the persons commonly called Christians, who were hated for their enormities. Christus, the name of the founder, was put to death by Pontius Pilate, procurator of Judea in the reign of Tiberius: but the pernicious superstition, repressed for a time broke out again, not only through Judea where the mischief originated, but through the city of Rome also (Annals xv 44).[183]

Tacitus had made a further reference to Christianity in a fragment of his histories, dealing with the burning of the Jerusalem temple in AD 70.

3. **LUCIAN OF SAMOSATA**: He was a satirist of the second century, who spoke scornfully of Christ and the Christians. He connected them with the synagogues of Palestine and alluded to Christ as ". . . the man who

---

[183] Ibid

was crucified in Palestine because he introduced this new cult into the world. Furthermore, their first lawgiver persuaded them that they were all brothers one of another after they have transgressed once for all denying the Greek gods and by worshipping that crucified sophist himself and living under his laws". Lucian also mentions the Christian several times in his "Alexander the false prophet."[184]

4. **PLINIUS SECUNDUS** (Pliny the Younger): Pliny, who was proprietor of Bithynia and Pontus in Asia Minor, wrote to Emperor Trajan about AD112 for advice as to how he should deal with Christians. His epistle gives valuable extra-biblical information concerning Christ. Pliny paid high tribute to the moral integrity of the Christians by writing of their unwillingness to commit theft or adultery, to falsify their word, or to repudiate a trust given to them. He went on to say that thing "sing a song to Christ as to a God". He wrote:

> They meet on a fixed day before dawn and sing responsively a hymn to Christ as to deity. They

---

[184] Ibid

bind themselves by oath . . . not to commit fraud, theft, or adultery, nor to falsify their trust, nor to refuse to return a trust when called upon to do so. When this is finished, it is their custom to dismiss and to assemble again to partake of food—ordinary and innocent food.[185]

5. **THE JEWISH TALMUDS**: Talmuds are commentaries on the law written by Jewish scholars from 100 to 500 AD. Several of these Talmuds have survived, including what is known as the Babylonian Talmud. Many of them contain direct, indirect and veiled reference to Jesus, His miracles, and even to his mother's virgin pregnancy.[186]

6. **THE QUR'AN**: Several places in the Quran give valuable information testifying to the birth, the death, the resurrection and the ascension of Jesus Christ. For example, sura chapter 3:45; 19:19-21 gives an account of the birth of Jesus Christ. Sura 19:33; 3:55 also talks about His death (although Muslims deny Christ's

---

[185] Pliny the Younger, *Letters, II*, books 8-10. Panegyricus, Loeb Classical Library, ed. B. Radice (Cambridge, MA: Harvard University, 1969), 10:96-97.

[186] Philip and Cherian, 11

death through crucifixion). Furthermore, sura 19:33 talks about His resurrection; sura 4:158 and 3:55 also talk about His ascension. The Qur'an affirms that He is in no way a mythical figure, but a real historical figure.

7. **THE NEW PRAJAPATI MOVEMENT:** In Hindu mythology, Prajapati is the primordial lord of creatures, and is mentioned in Vedic, epic and Puranic literature. He is described as the creator of the world, and the creator of heaven and earth in the Vedic legends. According to the advocates of this heresy, Prajapati, who is one of the 33 gods of the Vedas, is the Jesus Christ Himself.[187] Here is the point: though the above assertion is not true, yet the advocates of this teaching believe that there is a person in history called Jesus Christ which was why they identified with Him.

8. **OSSUARY OF JAMES:** In October of 2002, a limestone bone box dating to approximately 63 A.D was discovered in a Jerusalem cave. The box apparently once contained the bones of James, the brother of Jesus. Many scholars disputed the

---

[187] Ibid

authenticity of this discovery, claiming that the second part of the inscription, the portion which reads "brother of Jesus" to be a forgery. However, Joseph M. Holden reported:

> This indictment seems to have come to nothing after five years of court proceedings that concluded in March 2010 with 116 hearings, 138 witnesses, 52 expert witnesses, over 400 exhibits, and more than 12,000 pages of court transcripts! According to Golan's written summary of the trial (supported by the 474 page Hebrew language opinion handed down by Jerusalem District Court Judge Aharon Farkash on March 12, 2012), many high-level scholars with expertise in ancient epigraphy, paleography, bio-geology, and other crucial disciplines relating to examining the inscription have testified that there is no reason to doubt that the "brother of Jesus" was engraved by the same hand in the first-century A.D.[188]

The epigraphic report offers scientific evidence that the box is first century and the inscription has not been manipulated.

---

[188] Joseph M. Holden, *The James Ossuary: The Earliest Witness to Jesus and His Family?* http://normangeisler.com/the-james-ossuary-the-earliest-witness-to-jesus-and-his-family/ (accessed July 16, 2018).

9. **MAASAI PEOPLE IN THE SAVANNAS OF AFRICA:** The Maasai are indigenous African ethnic group of semi-nomadic people located in Kenya and northern Tanzania. In 1960, a creed was composed by the Maasai people in collaboration with missionaries from the congregation of the Holy Ghost as the declaration of their faith in Jesus Christ. The Maasai's Creed seems to be the African version of the Nicene Creed. The Maasai creed reads thus:

> We believe that God made good his promise by sending his Son, Jesus Christ, a man in the flesh, a Jew by tribe, born poor in a little village, who left his home and was always on safari doing good, curing people by the power of God, teaching about God and humanity, showing the meaning of religion is love. He was rejected by his people, tortured and nailed hands and feet to a cross, and died. He lay buried in the grave . . . and on the third day, he rose from the grave. He ascended to the skies. He is the Lord.[189]

Another controversy about Jesus' divine status is found in this question: Is Jesus the Mighty God or the Almighty God?

---

[189] J. Pelikan, "Maasai Creed," *America Public Media*, May 18, 2006, http://speakingoffaith.publicradio.org/programs/pelikan/masai.shtml (accessed September 13, 2019)

Is Jesus the Mighty God or the Almighty God?

A young man once sat in my Sunday school class on a Sunday morning. I had been told earlier by the person who invited him to our church that he was a member of the Jehovah's Witnesses. He came with his own version of Bible (the New Age Translation) and he paid rapt attention to all I had to say about Jesus. After teaching for a while, I asked him what he believed about Jesus and he boldly answered by saying Jesus is the mighty god while God the Father is the almighty God. I knew where he was coming from because I had earlier done an academic research on the Jesus of the Jehovah's Witnesses.

I asked the young man the reason for his belief and he referred me to Isaiah 9:6: " For unto us a child is born, unto us a son is given: and the government shall be upon his shoulder: and his name shall be called Wonderful, Counselor, *The mighty God*, The everlasting Father, the Prince of Peace". Having said that, I decided to cite passages in the Bible where God (Jehovah) was referred to as the Mighty God (see

Gen.49:24; Neh.9:32; Job 36:5; Ps.29:1; 50:1; Habakkuk 1:12; Isaiah 10:21; Luke 1:49) and in Revelation 1:8, Jesus was bold enough to call Himself the Almighty, a title reserved for God alone. Proponents of the view that Jesus is the mighty god and not the Almighty God claim that He is inferior to God the Father. This view is not true, in that, the scripture sometimes refer to God the Father as the Mighty God, while some places in the New Testament accords the title "The Almighty" to Jesus.

Is Jesus the mighty god or the almighty God? This actually sounds petty but it has generated serious arguments among some Christians and non-Christians. On one occasion Jesus said, "I and the Father are one" (John 10:30). He demonstrated several attributes that only God has. He forgave sins (Mark 2:5), healed the sick (Mark 2:11), He also demonstrated power over natural forces, stilled the raging storm of wind, raised the dead, and ultimately He resurrected from the dead. Christ's life moved and changed the course of history as only God could do. His life still greatly affect millions of souls around the world even after 2000 thousand years of His physical walk on earth. Drug addicts, terrorists, and cruel sinners have been transformed through the saving power of Jesus. Who could have done all these except the One who is the Almighty? Jesus is indeed the Almighty. He never tried to be like God; He is God Almighty Himself.

John Schaff sums up his picture of Jesus like this:

> This Jesus of Nazareth without money and arms, conquered more millions than Alexander, Caesar, Muhammad and Napoleon; without science and learning, he shed more light on matters human and divine than all philosophers and scholars combined; without the eloquence of schools, he spoke such words of life as were never spoken before or since and produced effects which lie beyond the reach of orator or poet; without writing a single line, he set more pens in motion and furnished themes for more sermons, songs of praise than the whole army of great men of ancient and modern times.[190]

Jesus Christ is not like other world leaders; He is not like Muhammad, Buddha, Alexander or Caesar. He is God. He is not the chairman of the board of

---

[190] Stott, Ibid

world leaders; He is God. He is not a lesser or inferior god; He is the Almighty God. Therefore, the greatest good that any man can do to others is to introduce them to Jesus as the Lord and the Savior of the whole world.

CHAPTER ELEVEN

Engaging the Intellectuals

Contrary to what some people think of Africa, Africa is not a jungle for baboons or the hub of illiteracy. There are intellectuals, great thinkers, men and women of substance, who are resourceful and creative in Africa.

There is a current intellectual inclination building up in Africa which is making Africans think for themselves and make intelligent choices and decisions. Africans are outgrowing religious gimmicks which once insulted their intelligence through religious dogmas and traditions. New ways of reasoning have been opened; there is unlimited access to learning; Africans have discovered for themselves, cure for the ancient intellectual deficiency that plagued them. Therefore, old traditions and practices are now summoned to strong intellectual scrutiny.

The intellectual breakthroughs Africans are experiencing in recent times have opened a new door for challenging traditions and religious systems that are antithetical to biblical Christianity— though this have both positive and negative effects on Christianity. In its positive sense, Christians are challenged to study the Bible for themselves. This in turn has helped to create logical resistance against heretical doctrines and practices in Africa.

In one of my Bible classes in a Seminary, I taught about the dangers of heresy in the church and how the ancient church authorities dealt with heretics. Along the line, I made mention of Giordano Bruno, the 16th century Italian philosopher and formal Catholic priest who were burned at the stake in 1600 for a stubborn adherence to his then unorthodox beliefs. After few minutes of discussion on the life of Bruno, I noticed one of my students nodded to show agreement. I became interested and I asked why she nodded, to my surprise, she told me openly that she just confirmed all I said about Bruno on her mobile device. That was the first time I saw a student going that far. I liked it because it helped me to be more conscious of the information I give, and I am happy because it is becoming a trend among young intellectuals in Africa. Africans are becoming like the Berean Christians who would always confirm what the apostles taught them.

However, this is not without a negative effect on the church. Some young intellectuals feel there is no need depending on clerics and trained exegetes to interpret the Bible to them, since they equally have access to 'unlimited' resources here and there to help them understand the Bible for themselves. This is good and it is true that God intended that the Bible will be understood by everybody, but is it clear from the Bible itself that there are some difficult passages that requires special skill to interpret—Ezra interpreted the Law to the remnants in Israel; Philip had to interpret the book of prophet Isaiah to the Ethiopian eunuch; Peter admitted that Paul's letters contain some things that are hard to understand. Therefore, in an attempt to secure 'interpretive independence', the Bible has been misinterpreted, under interpreted or over interpreted.

Furthermore, intellectual arrogance, bellicosity, unwholesome criticism, manipulation, rebellion and heresies are some of the negative effects resulting from the intellectual breakthroughs presently experienced in Africa. As a result, some biblical doctrines passed down by the orthodox fathers of the church have been rudely challenged. For instance, some Christian groups who thought they know better than the fathers of the church are calling for the abolition of water baptism and the Lord's Supper in the church, calling them 'irrelevant practices' in the church. Surprisingly, they also claimed to have drawn their arguments from the Bible. Attempts to correct them and help set the record straight have led to tongue lashing and they are rather belligerent.

Due to their quest to interpret the Bible for themselves without prior training in biblical interpretation and the help of experienced teachers of the word to guide them, these young intellectuals have consciously or unconsciously twisted the Bible, misled many, manipulated people's minds, and have even resorted to publishing propagandas against the church in order to gain 'cheap popularities'.

Therefore, there is need to engage the intellectuals with logical explanations for the Christian faith, not with an attempt to win the intellectual war existing between the intellectuals and Christianity in Africa, but to help expose the errors contained in their presuppositions and to establish the truth of the gospel. This will weaken their arguments against biblical Christianity, bible doctrines and ultimately help them find biblical answers to the rest of their quandaries. To achieve this feat, I recommend 'Analytical Method of Defense'.

Tools for Defending the Christian Faith

Scores of books have been written over the years by apologists to expose and refute errors against the Bible and generally the Christian faith. The nineteen fifties saw the rise of highly organized opposition to the Christian faith. The opponents formed numerous organizations worldwide, launched many bulletins, magazines, and journals and began capturing key seminaries and publishing houses of Christians. During this period, various techniques like propaganda, mind-manipulation, and debating were employed to attack the Christian faith.[191] Also in the last half of the twentieth century, the world witnessed the rise of specialization in every field of science, technology and social sciences. The tools used became refined and sophisticated that this idea became the norm in anti-Christian movements of this period. Radicals, atheists, and rationalists also developed specialized fields, techniques, and tools for attacking the Christian faith. Only an equal level of sophisticated and specialization in the apologetics camp could meet this new wave of assault.[192]

Interestingly in the 1980s, Johnson C. Philip of Calvin Research Group made the first attempt to develop specific tools for defending the Christian faith. He started an analysis of the sophisticated techniques used by the radicals and rationalists against the

---

[191] Afolabi, Ibid., 84

[192] Ibid

Christian faith. He also searched through the techniques used and proposed by Apologists before him. Results of these analyses, along with effective tools and strategies for counter-attack were then proposed by him in early 1980s through a large number of publications. These tools are what I referred to as *Analytical Method of Defense*. These tools include the following:

1. **Analysis of Errors of Interpretation**: Bible interpretation is one of the major functions of Christian Apologetics. Each book of the Bible needs to be interpreted in the light of its genre, the culture in which it was written and the values which it reflects. Analysis of errors of interpretation is a very important tool because many objections raised against the Bible are deeply rooted in thinking contrary to the Bible, which is what the secular mind does. These errors are analyzed and exposed with the help of this tool.[193]

2. **Analysis of Scripture Twisting**: Scripture twisting and errors of interpretation often look as though they

---

[193] Johnson C. Philip and Saneesh Cherian, *Tools for Integrated Apologetics: An Introduction* (India: Calvin Research Institute, 2003), 2

are the same, but they are different. Scripture Twisting is always deliberate and subtle while errors of interpretation are many times unintentional and cruder.[194] The apologist should know both, and he should counter them with appropriate answers.

3. **Analyzing Bible Difficulties:** Bible difficulties or contradictions are apparent in the Bible, and many skeptics and biblical antagonists are specialized in bringing up such contradictions as a means to attack the Bible.[195] Skeptics imply that the Bible is full of errors and difficulties, and therefore it cannot be a divinely inspired book. Sometimes these attacks undermine the faith of Christians who do not have the available resources to deal with the issue. This tool will help the apologist to handle such questions and deal effectively with even the most determined opponent.[196]

---

[194] Ibid

[195] Ibid

[196] Afolabi, Ibid., 87

It is important to note that the apparent contradictions in the Bible are copyists' errors, not errors from the original autographs. These errors occurred when copying the manuscripts. These errors sometimes occur when one word is improperly divided into two words. For example: changing "nowhere" into "now here". This is called "Fission". Other textual errors may occur, leading to contradictions, when there is dittography, fusion, haplography, homophony or metathesis. Some of these Bible difficulties are found in passages like Gen. 6:19-20 and Gen. 7:2-3; Gen. 5:24, 2Kings 2:11, Hebrews 11:5 and John 2:13.

Interestingly, none of the copyist errors present problems doctrinally. Therefore, when engaging intellectuals who specialize in bringing up contradictions as a means to attack the Bible, the apologist will do well to first analyze what the skeptics consider contradictions, examine the context, and apply the Law of non-contradiction to the texts. In most cases, these contradictions only occur in their understanding, not in the Bible itself.

5. **Analyzing Fallacies of Logic:** Errors and fallacies of logic have become powerful tools in the hands of the radicals. These tools are employed to attack the Bible and the Christian Apologist cannot counter these arguments without a basic background in formal logic.[197] This tool is an inevitable tool in the hands of any modern apologist if he must readily defend his faith that has been attacked through false logic and fallacies.[198] Understanding the use of all these tools will help in defending the Christian faith.

6. **Analysis of Propaganda Technique and Analysis of mind manipulation Techniques:** Analysis of propaganda and mind manipulation techniques among the tools of Apologetics provides the techniques and strategies needed to counter those who use propaganda and mind manipulation to attack the Christian faith.[199]

---

[197] Philip and Cherian, Ibid., 3

[198] Ibid

[199] Ibid

The rise of mass political movements and the rise of consumer economy in the 20th century made it necessary to refine propaganda and mind manipulation to a high level and those who fight against the Christian faith liberally make use of these techniques to attack the Christian faith.[200] Assertion is commonly used in modern propaganda.

Assertion is a passionate or energetic statement presented as a fact, although it is not necessarily true. It is one of the tools used by critics and propagandists to attack the Christian faith. It is therefore important for a serious apologist to know and understand the usage of these techniques so as to provide for him a more superior technique and strategies needed to counter and refute those who use propaganda and mind manipulation to attack the Christian faith.[201]

7. **Analysis of Debating Technique:** There is a settled notion in the minds of many that debating is a good way of bringing out truth. In the contrary, right from

---

[200] Afolabi, 88

[201] Ibid

the time of the Greek Sophists, pulpit-based public debates have been more a test of wits than truth. In the recent times, debate no longer strife to establish the truth but to test intelligence and skills.[202]

The mere skilled debater is always able to sway people to his side, irrespective of whether he is right or wrong. Debate these days are not fought over facts. They are fought for winning the war of ideas. Radicals and skeptics alike therefore employ the debating techniques to attack the Christian faith with the motive to make the unprepared and untrained apologist and Christian to sway from the faith he holds. The authors of the Calvin research group academic resources therefore warn that Christian Apologist should not take debates without first mastering this tool.[203]

8. **Analysis and Formulation of Leading Questions:** An interrogator can frame questions in such a way that the responder is automatically incriminated every

---

[202] Ibid

[203] Ibid

time irrespective of the answer.²⁰⁴ Questions like, "Did you stop beating your wife," "How fast was the red car going when it smashed into the blue car" falls into this category. Analyzing the two leading questions above, the former, in a subtle way, it raises the prospect that there is a problem between the man and his wife, while the latter implies that the red car was at fault, and the word "smashed" implies a high speed.

Radical thinkers and communicators have refined to a high degree the techniques for asking deceptive leading questions. Thus, the formulation of deceptive questions and the effective antidote to them should both be studied by the Christian apologist.²⁰⁵

In addition to the analytical methods suggested above, other valid methods are suggested below. These methods are relevant and practical methods which will, to a significant extent, bring inquirers and doubters to the point where they have to decide who to believe and what to believe about the Christian faith,

---

²⁰⁴ Ibid

²⁰⁵ Ibid

and then the Holy Spirit will complete the work of conviction and conversion in their hearts.

This is important because the goal of these methods is not to impose a belief on inquirers or coerce them to accepting the Christian faith. However, none of the methods suggested in this book is sacrosanct—they can be improved upon by others. Therefore, the following methods are suggested for defending the faith in Africa:

A. Method of Familiarization

Familiarization has to do with getting oneself acquainted to what others believe. It is one of the major and appropriate methods for defending the faith. This is very pertinent to the task of defending the faith because the apologist needs to know where his opponent or inquirer is coming from and why he has chosen to believe what he believes. It is wrong and unprofessional for an apologist to start condemning or refuting what he knows nothing about. A belief is already formed in the mind of the inquirer and simply telling the inquirer that what he or she believes is wrong shows lack of competence on the part of the apologist without first getting himself familiar with the presuppositions of his inquirer.

Why will a Muslim reject the doctrine of Trinity? Why is the deity of Jesus a problem to them? What are the points of disagreement between Christianity and other religions? These are some of the questions an apologist must avail himself to answer before approaching his opponents or inquirer, and this has to do with familiarizing oneself with the creeds and presuppositions of the opposing religions. Opposing presuppositions will have to be analyzed, tested, or shown to be false to prove or disprove their veracity. Understanding and analyzing the basic and prevailing presuppositions in various belief systems can greatly help an apologist in refuting opposing positions and this can only be done by familiarizing oneself with those presuppositions.

B. Method of Interaction

Interaction in this context means a conversation or exchange between two or more people. Applying this method implies that the apologist is not trying to assume the position of a superior fellow or coming with the disposition of instructing the opponent or his inquirer on what he or she should believe. Rather, it is a dialogue which bothers on clarifying and verifying what is the truth. This method allows the opponents or inquirers to present their views and in turn, the apologist, without compromise and with a sense of respect and meekness presents what he believes and why he has chosen to believe what he believes.

This method creates the atmosphere of friendliness and concentration, allows for meditation and also creates more rooms for questioning. However, there is the tendency for distractions and digression. Therefore, digression of the main subject of discussion must be avoided. The apologist must ensure that discussions which have no relevance to the subject are quickly discarded. Also, when applying this method, the apologist may request his opponent or inquirer to rephrase vague statement and make it clear enough. The apologist must correct wrong assertions and also keep the conversation simple and interactive. Furthermore, the apologist must avoid the use of jargons and verbiages, especially when opponents or inquirers do not belong to the same field with him.

C. Method of Verification of Truth Claims

The bone of contention is the truth every religion claims. The postmodern ideology claims that truth is relative. Therefore, since the postmodern ideology denies absolute truth, every religion claims personal truth. Interestingly, the immediate concern of Christian apologetics is to establish the *truth*, while its ultimate goal is the repentance of unbelievers (2Tim.2:25). Since postmodern ideology insists on relative truth and the Christian faith is built upon the absolute truth of God's word, there is bound to be some contentions. Ramm asserts: "Any claim for the truth of a religion appeals to some criterion or criteria. . . ."[206] The problem of truth is actually the bone of contention between Christianity and the opposing religions.

Contrary to Jesus' claims as "The Truth" in the gospel of John which shows absoluteness, Bunn's law states that, "All truth is relative to the perception of the individual". Bunn's law bluntly denies the

---

[206] Afolabi, 20

existence of any absolute truth, and this is the cardinal argument used by the opponents of Christianity today. The actual meaning of truth and the verification of its reality has become a major concern to many people through the past centuries. Pontius Pilate, the Roman governor of Judea and the magistrate upon which Jesus suffered and was crucified asked Jesus this same mind puzzling question: "What is Truth?" In spite of his Roman education and exposure, Pilate yet found it very difficult to answer this question of truth himself. Blaise Pascal maintains: "Truth is so obscure in these times, and falsehood so established, that, unless we love the truth, we cannot know it."[207]

Ramm declares: "All human disciplines must come to terms with truth, and the magnitude of the claims of at least the great historical religions demands that religion too come to terms with the problem of truth."[208] He added: "The first function of Christian

---

[207] Ibid., 25-6

[208] Ibid

apologetics is to show how the Christian faith is related to the claims".[209] Therefore, Christian apologetics is not interested in merely defending any Christian traditional heritage, but to reveal truth.

In summary, Carnell's submission remains that the concept of coherence in which logical self-consistency is coupled with agreement with the world of fact and experience is the most adequate and reliable tool for verifying truth. Truth is therefore whatever corresponds with the mind of God and is not self-contradictory because God by nature is self-consistent and He cannot err. Therefore, the final goal of Christian apologetics is to refute any form of distortion and attack leveled against the Christian faith by evidently presenting a reliable proof for its truth claims and ultimately establishing the actual truth.

D. The Method of Persuasion

Persuasion is the addressing of arguments to someone with the intention of changing their mind or convincing them of a certain point of view, course of

---

[209] Ibid

action etc. It is an argument or other statement intended to influence one's opinions or beliefs. This is one of the major relevant methods for defending the Christian faith in Africa. The duty of the apologist is to persuade inquirers or doubters to accept the Christian worldview. However, this method does not call for manipulation. It is a sincere persuasion of the inquirer with the intention of changing their mind or convincing them of the truth of Christianity.

This method is a way of appealing to the reasoning of the inquirer or doubters, without trying to manipulate their minds. Unhealthy compromise must be avoided when applying this method. The apologist must avoid poisoning the well, i.e. presenting negative information about a person before he/she speaks so as to discredit the person's argument.

In all, the logical fallacies of *ad hominem* (attacking the individual instead of the argument), *non sequitar* (comments or information that do not logically follow from a precise or the conclusion) must be avoided. Respect and meekness are key factors an apologist cannot afford to compromise. His goal is not to win an argument, but to establish the truth.

Means for Defending the Christian Faith in Africa

I have carefully selected the means relevant to defending the Christian faith in Africa to fit into the current global trend. The means for defending the faith in Africa includes:

A. Evangelism

Evangelism has been used over the years for communicating the Christian message to non-Christians. It could be personal or mass evangelism. Evangelism in itself is basically about persuading non-Christians to accept the Christian faith.

Evangelism as a New Testament activity carries the following idea:

1. Sharing one's experience with others
2. Talking to others
3. Telling others about Jesus
4. Teaching others the gospel systematically
5. Announcing the gospel to people can respond
6. Convincing others to follow Jesus

7. Driving home the gospel; in other word, meeting the people's needs
8. Answering reasonable objections
9. Persuading those who are hesitant.

In my opinion, every evangelistic endeavor must be apologetic in nature. It must seek to tell others about Jesus, convince others to follow Jesus, answer reasonable objections and to persuade those who are hesitant. An evangelist can function as an apologist on the field, telling his audience the reasons to accept the Christian faith. The evangelist must have a sound knowledge of the Christian faith, and be able to communicate same to his audience. However, since the focus of this section is evangelism, a little knowledge of African Evangelicalism will be beneficial.

Early missionary theology in Africa was by and large evangelical. Early missionary theology preached the necessity of faith in Jesus Christ as the only way to heaven. But this theology tended to be individualistic and other-worldly. Salvation was for the individual believer in heaven above. Early missionary theology tended to neglect this present world. The kingdom of God for them was the church. Therefore Christians should not get involved in politics since politics was worldly. Christianity was a Sunday religion. Christianity was about conversion of the soul, not the body.[210]

Contemporary African evangelicalism has put the Gospel into the modern context of poverty, suffering, unemployment and disease. African evangelicalism believes that Jesus is the answer to these problems. It is thus necessary to believe in Jesus as one's personal Savior. Faith in Jesus will guarantee eternal life in heaven. But faith in Jesus will also provide solutions to our problems on this earth.[211]

Paul Gifford writes:

> The popular Christianity we encountered [in Africa] . . . was not concerned with a renewed order or any 'new Jerusalem', but with a job, a husband, a child, a car, an education, a visa to the West. It was about succeeding in this realm." He says that the missionaries taught hardship in this life in exchange for happiness

---

[210] Timothy P. Palmer, *African Christian Theology: A New Paradigm* https://tcnn.ng/african-christian-theology-a-new-paradigm (accessed July 25, 2018)

[211] Ibid

hereafter. But "the missionary legacy has vanished with scarcely a trace, for it is terrestrial rewards that feature so prominently in African Christianity today.[212]

Furthermore, because of Africans' strong belief in the world of spirits, one of the major concerns of Africans is how they can be spiritually protected from any the attacks of the evil spirits or the spirit of witchcraft which they strongly believe are all out to harm them. In order to protect themselves, non-Christians would fortify themselves with charms, concoctions, incisions and sometimes offer sacrifices to the spirits so as to be in good terms with them.

On the other hand, Christians amongst the Africans are also not unaware of the possibility of spiritual attacks and demonic assaults on people. So they are equally on their guards against any form of spiritual attack, and in their quests to protect themselves or prevent any of such attack, they fortify themselves with warfare prayers and fasting, and also seek spiritual protections in churches where fervent

---

[212] Paul Gifford, *African Christianity: Its Public Role* (Bloomington: Indiana University Press, 1998), 339-40.

warfare prayers can be prayed for them. Those who feel they have been bewitched or oppressed and afflicted by these evil spirits would seek deliverance through prayers and special ministrations.

Therefore, the Jesus Africans would to accept and follow is the Jesus who will assure them of total protection from every form of demonic assault, help them overcome their spiritual enemies, alleviate their poverty, give them sound health, and generally make life easy for them. Consequently, the kind of evangelism that will thrive in Africa must include social welfare, where the gospel is not just spoken to the people, but also shown to them materially.

The evangelist may not necessarily be a professional apologist, but he must have some knowledge of apologetics, so that he is not bemused if confronted with questions which require logical explanations for his truth claims. However, no matter how arrogant and unruly his opponent is, the evangelist must never be arrogant.

B. Sound Biblical Interpretation

There is an urgent need for sound biblical interpretation. Lack of this has led the church in Africa into diversity of doctrines that are not consistent with the Scripture. The reason for sound biblical interpretation is because what each Christian understands about the bible affects every aspect of his Christian life i.e. his devotion, his prayers, his character, his perspectives to life, his worship, his interaction with others, his ideology, his dispositions and even his family relationship. The weaker believers become in their understanding of scriptures, the weaker they are spiritually and morally. Also, lack of scriptural understanding will certainly lead to wrong application of biblical truth.

Sound biblical interpretation will save the Church in Africa from error and will bring clarity to the scriptures and the Christian faith. Therefore, exegetical teaching of the Bible should be encouraged in churches all across Africa, so that both clergies and laities may be sound in the knowledge of God and His word and they may proclaim the same to others.

Heresy is almost inevitable where the Bible is not correctly understood and applied. Also, the widespread of syncretic practices which are totally foreign to biblical Christianity can be traced down to poor understanding of the scripture. Doctrinal diversities in the Church can also be traced back to how each denomination interprets the Bible.

The Bible is either misinterpreted, under-interpreted or over-interpreted before there can be error, and the three must be avoided. Therefore, the author maintains that sound biblical exegesis must be encouraged in the church, so that heresies can be reduced to the barest minimum. Contextual hermeneutics should be employed to drive home the biblical message to Africans.

D. The Use of Traditional and Social Media

The growing influence of traditional and social media in Africa can be used as a good tool to communicate the gospel message and to defend the Christian faith in Africa among its attackers. Young people are the best users of social media and they are also the most vulnerable. They interact more with the social media and they tend to accept the information they see on the social media, especially when the information comes from those they admire. They are easily tossed to and fro by every wave of doctrine and these strange doctrines are flung all across the social media.

Population estimate for Africa in 2019 is 1,320, 038,716, with 464,923,169 Internet users across Africa in December 2018, a 35.2% penetration rate.[213] In Nigeria alone, according to 2016 Nigeria Internet Statistics (usage compilation), Nigeria is among the ten countries with the most internet users in the world with the seventh position starting from China. Nigeria with a population of about 186,879,760 and 97,210,000 internet users reveal that about 52% of our population uses the internet. Facebook obtain up to 16 million users, meaning that about 8.6% of Nigerians are on Facebook.

The most visited websites in Nigeria are google.com, google.com.ng, facebook.com, youtube.com,

---

[213] *Internet World Stats*, https://www.internetworldstats.com/africa.htm (accessed September 11, 2019)

yahoo.com, twitter.com, jumia.com.ng, nairaland.com, linkedin.com,eskimi.com,instagram.com,wikipedia.org, konga.com, amazon.com, and vanguardngr.com among many others.[214] Apologists can leverage on the social media as one of the means for defending the faith. Facebook, Twitter, Instagram, Eskimi, Google plus, Youtube, and blog sites can provide amazing platform for reaching the unreached and debunking spurious doctrines.

Furthermore, the uses of traditional media like television, radio, and other periodicals can help as means for defending the faith in Africa. Film producers can deliberately produce movies with the aim of defending the Christian faith, like the movie titled *The Case for the Real Jesus* by Lee Strobel and many others. Also, television and radio programs can be centered on defending the Christian faith and answering reasonable objections.

---

[214]*Nigeria Internet Statistics* www.wbbclick.com.ng/nigeria-internet-statistics-nigerians-online/ (accessed September 27, 2017)

E. Publication of Literature

Deliberate effort must be made for the publication of literature, tracts and other literary works which bothers on defending the Christian faith in Africa. Although, several books have been written and published on the subject of apologetics, but only few are available to readers in Africa because the publication of such books have not really been encouraged on the continent.

History records that the early Church fathers wrote and published many apologetic works to defend the faith. Even from the apostolic era, publications were made to refute errors and to proclaim the truth. Paul wrote against Gnosticism, Luke and other evangelists wrote to tell the then world that Christianity is never against the state, that Christians are peacekeepers, and that Christianity is the only religious that brings man back to his Maker. John wrote against the heretic teachings of Cerinthus and Docetism. The second century fathers wrote and spoke against the erroneous doctrines of the Ebionites, and from the second to the fifth centuries of the Church, many apologetic works were published by the Church fathers to refute errors and vindicate Christianity as the true religion.

Apathy is dangerous to the well-being of Christianity in Africa. Heresies are receiving increasing media attentions and the Church has been silent about it. There is a widespread of heresies in the church today because no one seems to talk about them. Even among celebrated clergies and popular televangelists, heretical teachings are gaining recognition. One of the ways this can be tackled is for church leaders, scholars and Christian writers in Africa to venture into mass publications of apologetic and polemical literature.

In conclusion, apologetics and polemics must be given priority in Africa. The *rose-garden theology* which the church in Africa has adopted must not be a substitute for the scriptural command to contend earnestly for the faith. The church must never fold her arms and pretend not to know about the widespread of the heretical teachings which had led many astray already. The thrust of this book therefore is to awaken every Christian leader to the task of defending the

Christian faith, because the church will not only be judged for every idle word that proceeds from her mouth, but also for every idle silence.

CHAPTER TWELVE

The Jesus Africans Would Accept

The African continent has indeed been ravaged by political, social and economic instabilities, which has resulted in injustice, corruption, hostility, oppression, terrorism, and the destruction of lives and properties. Terrorists have rendered many families homeless, and millions of Africans are living in abject poverty and continuous suffering. There is high rate of unemployment on the continent; sicknesses and diseases have reduced the lives of many to nothing.

The problems of injustice, poverty, insecurity, social inequity, human trafficking, malnutrition, physical and sexual abuses, exploitation and bigotry are apparent on the continent of Africa. The numbers of refugees are increasing by the day. There are countless numbers of children on the streets, unable to get basic education, subject to malnutrition, physical and sexual assaults. These children also suffer many health risks from unhygienic living conditions and malnutrition.

A devastating consequence of the HIV/AIDS pandemic, felt most acutely in Africa, is the growing number of orphans left behind when parents die in the prime of their lives. The figures are staggering. Africa is home to at least 12 million orphans today, with rapid increases projected into the foreseeable future. A far larger group of children are affected by HIV-related illness among their parents, siblings, and community. As many as 2 million African children are themselves HIV positive or suffer from AIDS.[215]

Some territories have become uninhabitable for people due to the activities of terrorists. Africa is also faced with the problem of religious intolerance which has equally resulted in some sort of religious conflict on the continent. Some terrorists under the guise of herdsmen seeking for grazing zones have turned themselves to raving wolves, destroying lives and properties without mercy.

---

[215] Katherine Marshall & Marisa Van Saanen, *Development And Faith: Where Mind, Heart, And Soul Work Together* (Washington DC: The international Bank Reconstruction/The World Bank, 2007), 177

The world was alarmed at the abduction of the over 200 Chibok girls in Borno state of Nigeria and "Bring Back Our Girls" was chorused all over the world as a passionate campaign for their release. Few years after this, the world was alarmed again at the abduction of the over 100 Dapchi girls. Although a good number of the Dapchi girls were released shortly after their abduction, while some lost their lives and some are still in the custody of the abductors— especially a Christian girl, Leah Sharibu, who refused to renounce her faith in Christ. All of these speak of the level of insecurity in Africa, especially in Nigeria.

Although the federal government of Nigeria claimed to have tackled Boko Haram insurgency, and we must sincerely credit them for their efforts, but the activities of the herdsmen are equally *Bokoharamic*[216] in nature.

---

[216] Boko Haram is a known Islamic terrorist group in Nigeria, responsible for the killing of thousands of people and the abduction of the Chibok girls in Borno state, Nigeria. The author deliberately used the adjective "Bokoharamic" to describe any activity similar to that of the Boko Haram, which includes the destruction of properties, abduction, terrorism, violence, use of riffles to attack and kill people, forceful occupation of territories not belonging to them and any form of hostile activity which threatens communal peace.

Burning down people's properties and the use of riffles to attack the victims of their aggressions is purely *Bokoharamic*. Sadly, the Nigerian government is yet to find lasting solution to all these social menace.

The rate of unemployment on the continent is also of great concern. Citizens do not have access to good health care and many who could afford to pay the bills would rather go on a medical tourism to Europe and America. Many university and college graduates are underemployed, while millions of others fall into the category of the unemployed.

Other problems Africans battle with are infant mortality, malnutrition of children, lack of adequate care for the senior citizens, devaluation of human lives, religious and ethnic violence, armed robberies, starvation, exploitation of the poor, Judicial and economic corruption, *wanton governance*—a governance full of exploitation, self-centeredness, perjury and heartless greed—nepotism, bribery, perversion of justice, and lot more.

Obviously, the African continent is blessed with amazing natural and human resources, but the proceeds from these natural resources that could have greatly enriched the continent and make life better for the people were diverted into the personal treasuries of some corrupt leaders in Africa, and some funds were even mismanaged and misappropriated. Although, some African leaders have distinguished themselves and exonerated themselves from any form of accusation, but majority of political, traditional, and even religious leaders have some questions to answer.

Sadly, the generation of these corrupt leaders has also passed on the *legacy of corruption* to generations after them. No wonder young people who want quick riches but are not willing to work for it are getting themselves involved in cyber-crimes, fraud, and even money rituals.

Furthermore, as mentioned earlier, Africans believe in the world of the spirit. Apart from all the socio-political and economic challenges alighted above, Africans believe that there are also many spiritual forces to contend with. These forces of darkness may be responsible for automobile accidents, infertility, sicknesses, death, divorce, backwardness and other unfortunate situations. All these experiences are real to Africans, and this is why any Christian denomination whose ministerial emphasis is on economic and spiritual freedom thrives more in Africa.

Therefore, the Jesus Africans would likely embrace is the Jesus who could make the poor rich, heal the sick and also guarantee sound health, protect from harm, defend the defenseless, give power to overcome one's spiritual enemy and overpower the forces of darkness militating against the wellbeing of the people.

Jesus must be presented to Africans as the Savior who is sensitive to their needs, who sympathizes with those who are suffering, who is willing to identify with them in their needs and struggles, and who is coming again to end all life's struggles. Without diminishing any aspect of the gospel, the gospel of Jesus the Savior must be contextualized to accommodate African experiences and realities.

Naming Jesus among Africans

Following are the ways of naming Jesus among Africans:

- A liberator (and from one speaking within a Bakongo perspective, a 'Nvuluzy' i.e., a liberator, rescuer)
- My elder or eldest brother
- Proto-Ancestor or Ancestor
- Friend, 'Enyioma' (good friend)
- Healer (and from within the Bakongo perspective a 'Nganga-Nkisa' or healer)
- A great teacher
- Savior (or more specifically, 'Chinazo', which means 'God saves', in Igbo)
- Neighbor (one and one for the following as well),
- A guest who is open to friendship,
- A new Moses,
- Within an Igbo context, Jesus as one's true chi,
- One who is present and walks with me,
- One whose life explains my own life ('okowandum', among the Igbos),
- One who purifies cultures,
- The best illustration of a genuine relationship,

- Alpha and Omega ('Ejesia ogu', among the Igbos),
- The Christ of Hope,
- Jesus, my Providence,
- Jesus, the compassionate, the co-sufferer.[217]

The above names are the reflections of the images of Christ in African theology. Jesus is seen as an ancestor or proto-ancestor, healer, brother, liberator, and King. Therefore, the apologetic endeavor that will thrive in Africa must present Jesus as the Savior who protects, heals spiritually, physically and emotionally. He must be presented as the true mediator between man and his Creator, the one who will ultimately end all tribal conflicts, the one who will liberate from poverty, demonic oppressions, pains, and the one who cares for and defend the poor. In other words, more of functional than ontological Christology is what Africans need.

Donald J. Goergen opined:

> The nations of Africa have been wounded by the slave trade, colonization, the post-colonial formation of the nation-States, neo-colonialism's

---

[217] Donald J. Goergen, *The Quest for the Christ of Africa.* https://sedosmission.org/old/eng/goergen.htm (accessed July 24, 2018)

economic dependency, intertribal violence and war, the corruption of many post-independence national leaders, and so on. Could not the healing Jesus have a strong appeal in Africa today? Is he not what Africa needs now more than ever?[218]

There is Hope for Africa

Africa shall rise again and her glory shall break forth. Africans shall someday experience good governance, her people shall be known for integrity and moral uprightness, justice, equity, and peace. Her borders shall once again be secured, free from the intrusion of cruel invaders. The displaced and refugees shall someday return home, and children shall embrace their parents again in conviviality. Everyone shall live peacefully and all tribal and ethnic conflicts shall cease.

Children on the street shall return home to enjoy good parenting and get good education. Knowledge shall increase—especially the knowledge of God—and true Christianity shall be embraced. Africa shall once again return to sound biblical exegesis, free from

---

[218] Ibid

heresies, Christocentric in character and life transforming in nature.

The season of famine of sound biblical exegesis is coming to its end and there shall be revival of the Word of God, where the scripture is allowed to speak for itself. In this fast approaching season of theological and exegetical revival in Africa, there shall emerge the true seekers of the face of God and not only the seekers of the hand of God. African Christology shall embrace ontological and functional Christology in perfect balance. Africa is blessed, African is a blessing and African shall be blessed forever and ever (Amen).

CHAPTER THIRTEEN

My Recommendations

In view of all the previous discussions on Christian apologetics and its need in Africa, I hereby offer the following recommendations to church leaders, Bible colleges, theological institutions, media personnel, journalists, and Christian educators:

A. To Church Leaders

1. Church leaders must endeavor to teach the church the core message of the gospel with total integrity and absolute dependence on the Holy Spirit. This suggests that the leaders must first be grounded in the word of God and must be sound in biblical interpretation and application. This therefore will help church leaders to correctly teach the church sound biblical doctrine, which is very important to the task of defending the

faith, because no one can correctly and adequately defend what he does not know.

2. Church leaders should see apologetics as part of their ministerial duties, because it is a mandate given to the church. The church leaders should equip themselves with the knowledge of apologetics and polemics, presuppositions and worldviews of other religious groups.

3. Church leaders who run Bible Colleges in their denominations should endeavor to include Christian apologetics in the college curriculum.

4. Church leaders should as well find out what their followers actually believe about the Bible, Jesus, Holy Spirit and the Christian faith in general. In doing this, church leaders will be able to know the stand of their followers about the Bible and the Christian faith, as this will make leaders to make necessary corrections when there is need for such.

5. Church leaders are enjoined to review their denominational tenets and confirm if they agree with the Scripture, so that they will no longer operate in error and by so doing lead others astray.

6. Christian leaders must always be ready to defend the faith within or outside the church with the use of either voice or pen.

7. Christian Apologetics Education should be introduced to the church and incorporated into the Christian education curriculum of the church.

B. To Christian Journalists

1. Christian journalists are at a very good advantage to present the truth and expose errors through the publication of Christian Journals.

2. Christian journalists must see apologetics and polemics as the collective responsibility of every Christian, irrespective of their professions.

3. The focus of Christian journalism should therefore be centered on Jesus and the Holy Scriptures.

4. It is therefore important for every Christian Journalists to understand the necessity of getting involved in Christian apologetics and learn how to use the tools suggested in this book.

C. To Christian Media Personnel

1. Christian media presenters should also consider apologetics as their responsibilities and therefore take

advantage of their professions to defend the Christian faith against attacks and doctrinal distortions.

2. The above point is therefore possible when Christian media personnel see apologetics as the duty of all Christians and not only for clergies.

3. Media presenters can achieve this by hosting programs that will educate the viewers on the core doctrines of Christianity and it can also be achieved by hosting notable, experienced and knowledgeable Christian leaders to explain the essential doctrines of the Bible.

D. To Seminaries and Bible Colleges

1. No theological seminaries and Bible colleges should ignore the study of Christian apologetics in their respective institutions, because they are in the best position to equip believers on how to defend the faith.

2. Seminaries and Bible colleges should focus their attentions not only on the theoretical aspects of apologetics, but they should be as pragmatic as possible.

3. Seminary and Bible College lecturers must not fail to educate students on the right way to defend the

faith, so that students do not jeopardize the real essence of the task.

4. Conscious effort must be made to present Christian apologetics from the African perspective.

E. To all Christians

1. Apologetics is a mandate for all Christians in every age. Therefore, Christians must wake up to the task of defending their most holy faith.

2. Finally, this book is recommended to be used as a study and reference material for students of theology, upcoming apologists, pastors, Christian educators, Christian writers, Bible teachers and other church leaders across Africa and the world.

BIBLIOGRAPHY

Afolabi, Ebenezer. *Defending What You Believe*. USA: Createspace, an amazon.com company, 2014.

Anderson, J.N.D *Christianity: The Witness of History*. London: Tyndale Press, 1969.

Barclay, William. *The Daily Study Bible: The Letters of James and Peter*. Edinburgh: The Saint Andrew Press, 1979.

Biggs, Charles A. *A Critical and Exegetical Commentary on the Epistles of St. Peter and St. Jude*. New York: Charles Scribner's Sons, 1901

Brewer, C. G *Contending for the Faith*. Tennessee: Gospel Advocate Company, 1941

Bruce, F.F. *First-century Faith*. Leicester: Inter-Varsity Press, 1977

Butler, Trent C. ed., *Holman Illustrated Bible Dictionary*. Nashville, USA: Thomas Nelson Publishers, 2003.

Carnell, Edward John. *An Introduction to Christian Apologetics*. Grand Rapids, MI: Eerdmans, 1948.

Cheung, Vincent. *Presuppositional Confrontations*. USA: Reformation Ministries International, 2003.

Easton, M.G. *Easton's Bible Dictionary*. USA: Books for the Ages, 1997.

Farinaccio, Joseph R. *Faith with Reason*. New Jersey: Bookspecs Publishing, 2002.

Geisler, Norman. *Baker Encyclopedia of Christian Apologetics*. Grand Rapids: Baker Books, 1999.

Geisler, Norman L. and William E. Nix, *From God to Us*. Chicago: Moody Press, 1974.

Grudem, Wayne. *Tyndale New Testament Commentary: 1 Peter*. Michigan: William B. Eerdmans Publishing Company, 1989.

Hastings, James ed., *The Speaker's Bible: I Peter, II Peter and Jude*. Great Britain: Speaker's Bible Office, 1924.

Hiebert, D. Edmond. *1 Peter*. USA: BMH Books, 1992.

Holmes, Michael W. ed., *Greek New Testament: SBL Edition*. Atlanta: Society of Biblical Literatures, 2010

Horton, David. *The Portable Seminary*. Michigan: Bethany House Publishers, 2006

Kenneth L. Barker and John R. Kohlenberger III. *Expositor's Bible Commentary*. Grand Rapids, Michigan: Zondervan, 1994

Little, Paul E. *Know Why You Believe*. Illinois: Intervarsity Press, 1988

Marshal, Katherine and Marisa Van Saanen. *Development And Faith: Where Mind, Heart, And Soul Work Together.* Washington DC: The International Bank Reconstruction/The World Bank, 2007.

Mbiti, John S. *African Religions and Philosophy.* London: Heinemann, 1969

McDowell, Josh. *A Ready Defense.* Nashville: Thomas Nelson Publishers, 1993.

McDowell, Josh and Sean McDowell, *Jesus: Dead or Alive?* California: Regal, 2009.

Metzger, Bruce M. *A Textual Commentary on the Greek New Testament.* New York: United Bible Societies, 1971.

Nichol, Francis D. gen. ed., *The Seventh-day Adventist Bible Commentary,* vol. 6,"The Holy Bible With Exegetical and Expository Comment", Washington D.C.: Review and Herald Publishing Association, 1980.

Stott, R. W. John. *Basic Christianity.* Downers Grove, III: InterVarsity Press, 1958.

Strobel, Lee. *The Case for Christ.* USA: Zondervan, 2007.

Strobel, Lee and Garry Poole, *Exploring The Da Vinci Code* (Grand Rapids, Michigan: Zondervan, 2006.

Philip, Johnson C. and Saneesh Cherian. *Introduction to Integrated Christian Apologetics.* India: A Calvin Research Group Academic Resource, 2003.

———, *Branches of Apologetics*. India: A Calvin Research Group Academic Resource, 2003.

Pliny the Younger, *Letters, II*, books 8-10. Panegyricus, Loeb Classical Library, ed. B. Radice (Cambridge, MA: Harvard University, 1969), 10:96-97.

Ramm, Bernard L. *A Christian Appeal to Reason*. Irving, Texas: International Correspondence Institute, 1968.

Rodríguez, Ángel Manuel. *What is Apostasy?* Biblical Research Institute General Conference of Seventh-day Adventists.

Thesis

Strickland, Melissa A. *The History of Christianity in Nigeria: A Case Study with Special Emphasis on the Southern Baptist Mission* (Thesis, Bachelor of General Studies, Texas Tech University), 1999.

Unpublished Work

Adeogun, Ebenezer *Notes on Apologetics*, (LIFE Theological Seminary Ikorodu, M.Th. Programme, Ikorodu Lagos, February), 2017.

Lecture Note on Church History. *The Advent and Expansion of Christianity in West Africa* (Nigeria: The Redeemed Christian Bible College), 2003.

Internet Resources

Anonymous. *Apologia.* https://en.m.wikipedia.org/wiki/Apologia.(accessed August 11, 2017).

Cheung, Vincent. *Commentary on First Peter* http://www.vincentcheung.com.pdf, (accessed June 26, 2017).

Christianity in Nigeria. https://en.wikipedia.org/wiki/Christianity_in_Nigeria (accessed September 8, 2017).

Clarke, Adam *Commentary on the Bible: 1 Peter Chapter 3.* http://www.sacredtexts.com/bib/cmt/clarke/pe1003.htm (accessed September 16, 2017).

Constable, Thomas L. *Notes of Jude.* https://www.soniclight.com, (accessed August 21, 2017).

_____. *Notes on 1 Peter.* https://www.ccbiblestudy.org (accessed July 25, 2018).

Goergen, Donald J. *The Quest for the Christ of Africa.* https://sedosmission.org/old/eng/goergen.htm (accessed July 24, 2018).

Guinness, O.S. *A Biblical Basis for Apologetics.* https://www.bethinking.org/apologetics/the-essence-of-apologetics/2-biblical-basis (accessed July 12, 2017).

Holden, Joseph M. *The James Ossuary: The Earliest Witness to Jesus and His Family?* http://normangeisler.com/the-james-ossuary-the-earliest-witness-to-jesus-and-his-family/ (accessed July 16, 2018).

Palmer, Timothy P. *African Christian Theology: A New Paradigm* https://tcnn.ng/african-christian-theology-a-new-paradigm (accessed July 25, 2018).

Pelikan, J. "Maasai Creed," *America Public Media*, May 18, 2006, http://speakingoffaith.publicradio.org/programs/pelikan/masai.shtml (accessed September 13, 2019).

Piper, John. *Contending for the Faith.* http://www.sermoncentral.com (accessed August 31, 2017).

Robinson, Maurice A. and William G. Pierpont, *The New Testament in the Original Greek Byzantine Text form,* ed. 2005. London: www.bibles.org.uk (accessed 16th of August, 2017).

Slick, Matt. *Logical Problem with the Michael Becoming Jesus Who Became Michael Again.* https://carm.org/logical-problem-with-angel-michael-become-jesus-beome-michael (accessed July 24, 2018).

Stedman, Ray. *Contending for the Faith.* http://www.sermoncentral.com (accessed August 31, 2017).

Utley, Bob. *Free Bible Commentary: Jesus' Half-Brothers speak: James and Jude.* www.freebiblecommentary.org (accessed 23, August, 2017).

William Barclay's Daily Study Bible. https://m.studylight.org/commentaries (accessed September 17, 2016)

Versions of the Bible

NIV Study Bible, *Introduction: 1 Peter*. Grand Rapids, Michigan: Zondervan, 2002.

The Holy Bible: New Revised Standard Version. New York: Thomas Nelson & Sons, 1989.

Author's Contact Information

Ebenezer Afolabi is a pastor, a worship leader, a conference speaker, a counselor, an apologist and a Bible teacher. He lectures in one of the study centers of LIFE Theological Seminary, West Africa.

To invite Ebenezer Afolabi to speak in your conference, symposium, seminar or convention, revival or retreat, please write to:

Foursquare Gospel Church

210 Ebute Ojora Street,

Ebute Road, Ibafo Ogun State

Nigeria.

Phone: +2349050586045

Email: ebenezerafolabi54@gmail.com

Facebook: www.facebook.com/damilola.afolabi

WhatsApp: +2348160525695

OTHER BOOKS BY THE AUTHOR

Careless Wives, Unfaithful Husbands.

List Price
Kindle: $2.99
Paperback: $8.00
ISBN-13:978-1537441818
Available at www.amazon.com
BISAC: Family & Relationships/ Marriage & Long Term Relationship

Women Marrying Younger Men: A Biblical Perspective

Available in kindle and paperback

Visit www.amazon.com for your copy

CPSIA information can be obtained
at www.ICGtesting.com
Printed in the USA
LVHW041418111119
636960LV00003B/680/P